Vanessa-Ann's

# Holidays In Cross-Stitch

## 1994

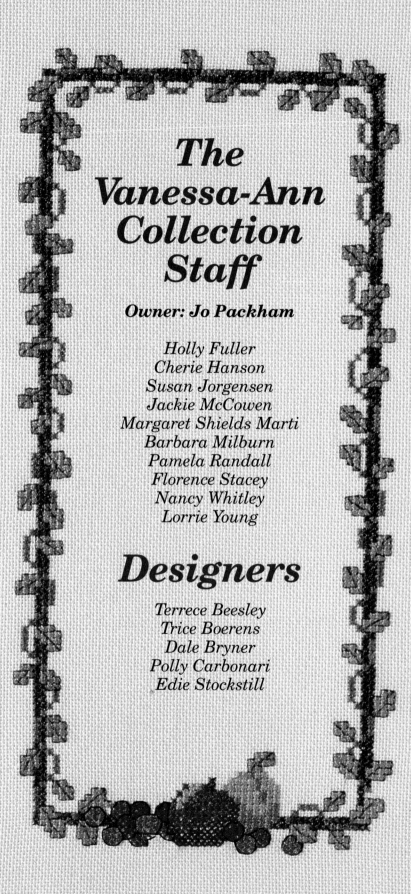

# The Vanessa-Ann Collection Staff

**Owner: Jo Packham**

Holly Fuller
Cherie Hanson
Susan Jorgensen
Jackie McCowen
Margaret Shields Marti
Barbara Milburn
Pamela Randall
Florence Stacey
Nancy Whitley
Lorrie Young

# Designers

Terrece Beesley
Trice Boerens
Dale Bryner
Polly Carbonari
Edie Stockstill

Vanessa-Ann's

# Holidays In Cross-Stitch

## 1994

©1993 by Oxmoor House, Inc.
Book Division of Southern Progress Corporation
P.O. Box 2463, Birmingham, AL 35201

Library of Congress Catalog Number: 86-62285
Hardcover ISBN: 0-8487-1137-8
Softcover ISBN: 0-8487-1417-2
ISSN: 0890-8230
Manufactured in the United States of America
First Printing 1993

Editor-in-Chief: Nancy J. Fitzpatrick
Senior Homes Editor: Mary Kay Culpepper
Senior Editor, Editorial Services: Olivia Kindig Wells
Director of Manufacturing: Jerry Higdon
Art Director: James Boone

*Holidays In Cross-Stitch 1994*

Editor: Lelia Gray Neil
Editorial Assistants: Patricia Weaver, Janica Lynn York
Copy Editor: L. Amanda Owens
Copy Assistant: Leslee Rester Johnson
Production Manager: Rick Litton
Associate Production Manager: Theresa L. Beste
Production Assistant: Marianne Jordan
Assistant Art Director: Cynthia R. Cooper
Designer: Diana Smith Morrison
Computer Artists: Kelly Davis, Carol Loria,
   Karen Tindall Tillery
Photographers: Ryne Hazen, John O'Hagan
Framer: Artist Touch

*The Vanessa-Ann Collection* offers heartfelt thanks to Susan Rios in Glendale, California; to Every Blooming Thing in Salt Lake City, Utah; to Anita Louise at Bearlace Cottage in Park City, Utah; to Mary Gaskill at Trends and Traditions in Ogden, Utah; and to Penelope Hammons in Layton, Utah, for allowing us to photograph on their premises. We sincerely appreciate their trust and cooperation.

**1994**

# Contents

**A**t The Vanessa-Ann Collection, we think of families and friends as beautiful threads stitched throughout our lives. They lend our days color, texture, and strength. Many of the things we stitch we make for them.

We bring you a year's worth of new designs to create for the people you love. Draw inspiration from this new edition of Holidays In Cross-Stitch.

page 36

*Delight someone you know with our Pink Blossom Bunny—just perfect for children of all ages. Our pages are filled with new favorites like this.*

## JANUARY

# *National Soup Month*

*What better time than blustery January to celebrate National Soup Month? As this piece charmingly affirms, a warm bowl of nourishing soup can be a "bear" necessity! Appropriate in the kitchen, this happy design would also be right at home in a child's playroom.*

# Soup's On

## SAMPLE
Stitched on white Jobelan 28 over 2 threads, the finished design size is 11⅞" x 8⅝". The fabric was cut 18" x 15".

| FABRICS | DESIGN SIZES |
|---|---|
| Aida 11 | 15⅛" x 10⅞" |
| Aida 14 | 11⅞" x 8⅝" |
| Aida 18 | 9¼" x 6⅝" |
| Hardanger 22 | 7⅝" x 5½" |

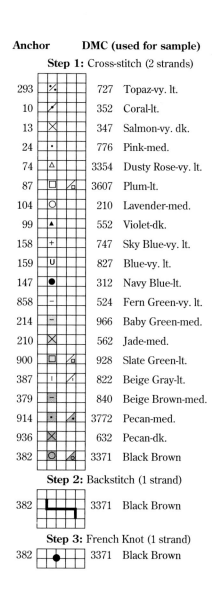

| Anchor | | DMC | (used for sample) |
|---|---|---|---|
| **Step 1:** Cross-stitch (2 strands) | | | |
| 293 | | 727 | Topaz-vy. lt. |
| 10 | | 352 | Coral-lt. |
| 13 | | 347 | Salmon-vy. dk. |
| 24 | | 776 | Pink-med. |
| 74 | | 3354 | Dusty Rose-vy. lt. |
| 87 | | 3607 | Plum-lt. |
| 104 | | 210 | Lavender-med. |
| 99 | | 552 | Violet-dk. |
| 158 | | 747 | Sky Blue-vy. lt. |
| 159 | | 827 | Blue-vy. lt. |
| 147 | | 312 | Navy Blue-lt. |
| 858 | | 524 | Fern Green-vy. lt. |
| 214 | | 966 | Baby Green-med. |
| 210 | | 562 | Jade-med. |
| 900 | | 928 | Slate Green-lt. |
| 387 | | 822 | Beige Gray-lt. |
| 379 | | 840 | Beige Brown-med. |
| 914 | | 3772 | Pecan-med. |
| 936 | | 632 | Pecan-dk. |
| 382 | | 3371 | Black Brown |
| **Step 2:** Backstitch (1 strand) | | | |
| 382 | | 3371 | Black Brown |
| **Step 3:** French Knot (1 strand) | | | |
| 382 | | 3371 | Black Brown |

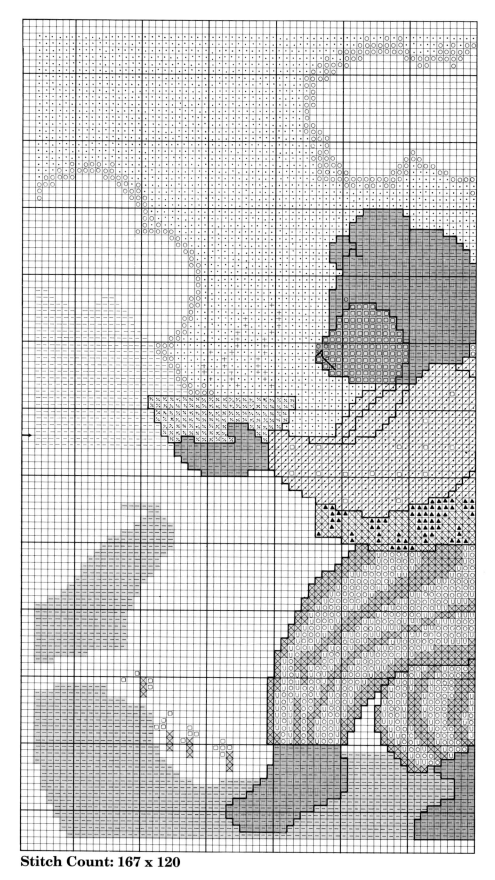

**Stitch Count: 167 x 120**

11

# Quilter's Escape

*The town of
Fond du Lac, Wisconsin,
sets aside the first weekend
in February to celebrate
the best in fabric arts.
Quilter's Escape
offers classes and
displays quilts and other
handcrafts. This sampler
combines a delightful
alphabet with a classic
quilt pattern, saluting
both cross-stitch
and quilting.*

# Stitcher's Delight

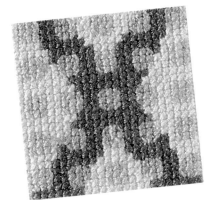

### SAMPLE
Stitched on white Murano 30 over 2 threads, the finished design size is 8⅝" x 13¼". The fabric was cut 15" x 20". See page 140 for framing ideas.

| FABRICS | DESIGN SIZES |
|---------|--------------|
| Aida 11 | 11⅞" x 18" |
| Aida 14 | 9¼" x 14⅛" |
| Aida 18 | 7¼" x 11" |
| Hardanger 22 | 5⅞" x 9" |

**(Graph continued on next page.)**

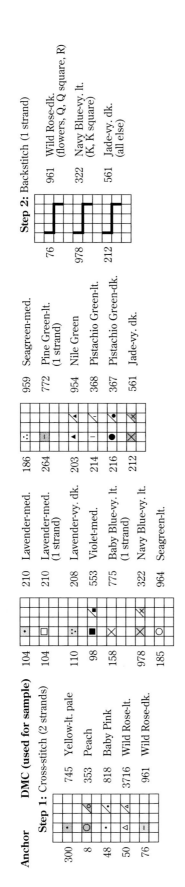

| Anchor | DMC (used for sample) |
|---|---|

**Step 1:** Cross-stitch (2 strands)

| | | Anchor | | DMC | |
|---|---|---|---|---|---|
| · | 300 | | 745 | Yellow-lt. pale |
| ○ | 8 | | 353 | Peach |
| ∕ | 48 | | 818 | Baby Pink |
| △ | 50 | | 3716 | Wild Rose-lt. |
| − | 76 | | 961 | Wild Rose-dk. |

| | | | | |
|---|---|---|---|---|
| · | 104 | 210 | Lavender-med. |
| □ | 104 | 210 | Lavender-med. (1 strand) |
| ∴ | 110 | 208 | Lavender-vy. dk. |
| ■ | 98 | 553 | Violet-med. |
| ✕ | 158 | 775 | Baby Blue-vy. lt. (1 strand) |
| ✕ | 978 | 322 | Navy Blue-vy. lt. |
| ○ | 185 | 964 | Seagreen-lt. |

| | | | | |
|---|---|---|---|---|
| ∷ | 186 | 959 | Seagreen-med. |
| ▬ | 264 | 772 | Pine Green-lt. (1 strand) |
| ◢ | 203 | 954 | Nile Green |
| ∕ | 214 | 368 | Pistachio Green-lt. |
| ● | 216 | 367 | Pistachio Green-dk. |
| ✕ | 212 | 561 | Jade-vy. dk. |

**Step 2:** Backstitch (1 strand)

| 76 | 961 | Wild Rose-dk. (flowers, Q, Q square, R) |
|---|---|---|
| 978 | 322 | Navy Blue-vy. lt. (K, K square) |
| 212 | 561 | Jade-vy. dk. (all else) |

Stitch Count: 130 x 198

# Carrot Festival

*Holtville, California, hosts an annual Carrot Festival that commemorates its abundant crop with a cooking contest, a parade, and an art show. Like the festival, the fresh colors in this piece will bring a taste of spring to a winter day.*

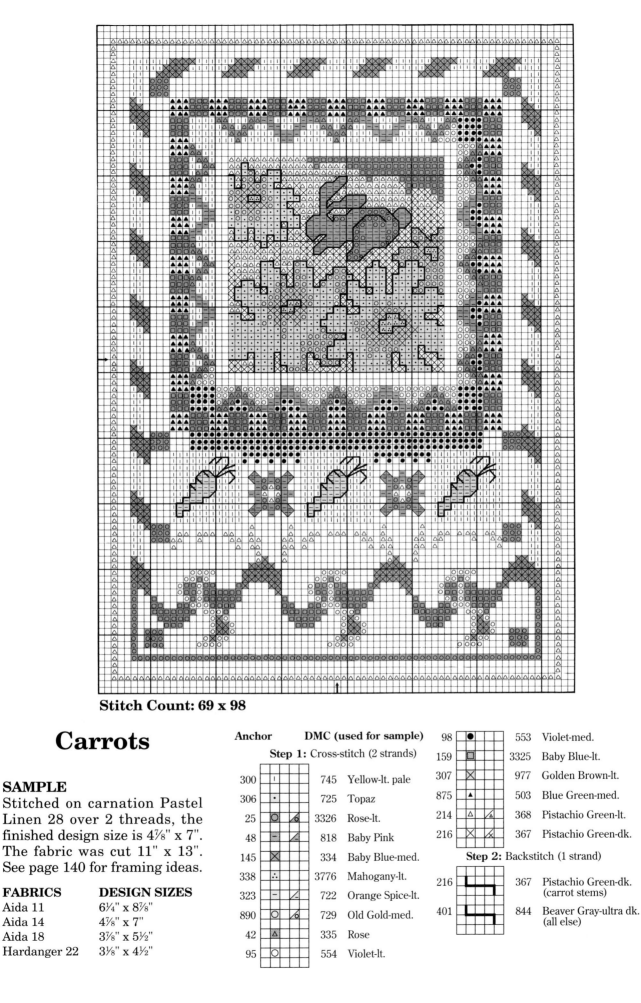

**Stitch Count: 69 x 98**

# Carrots

**SAMPLE**
Stitched on carnation Pastel Linen 28 over 2 threads, the finished design size is 4⅞" x 7". The fabric was cut 11" x 13". See page 140 for framing ideas.

| FABRICS | DESIGN SIZES |
|---|---|
| Aida 11 | 6¼" x 8⅞" |
| Aida 14 | 4⅞" x 7" |
| Aida 18 | 3⅞" x 5½" |
| Hardanger 22 | 3⅛" x 4½" |

| Anchor | | DMC (used for sample) | |
|---|---|---|---|
| | | **Step 1:** Cross-stitch (2 strands) | |
| 300 | | 745 | Yellow-lt. pale |
| 306 | | 725 | Topaz |
| 25 | | 3326 | Rose-lt. |
| 48 | | 818 | Baby Pink |
| 145 | | 334 | Baby Blue-med. |
| 338 | | 3776 | Mahogany-lt. |
| 323 | | 722 | Orange Spice-lt. |
| 890 | | 729 | Old Gold-med. |
| 42 | | 335 | Rose |
| 95 | | 554 | Violet-lt. |

| Anchor | | DMC | |
|---|---|---|---|
| 98 | ● | 553 | Violet-med. |
| 159 | | 3325 | Baby Blue-lt. |
| 307 | | 977 | Golden Brown-lt. |
| 875 | ▲ | 503 | Blue Green-med. |
| 214 | | 368 | Pistachio Green-lt. |
| 216 | | 367 | Pistachio Green-dk. |

**Step 2:** Backstitch (1 strand)

| Anchor | | DMC | |
|---|---|---|---|
| 216 | | 367 | Pistachio Green-dk. (carrot stems) |
| 401 | | 844 | Beaver Gray-ultra dk. (all else) |

## FEBRUARY 12–27

# *Winter Olympics*

**As the world joins hands this year
in Lillehammer, Norway, for the exciting
Olympic Games, you can show your enthusiasm
with this colorful sweatshirt.**

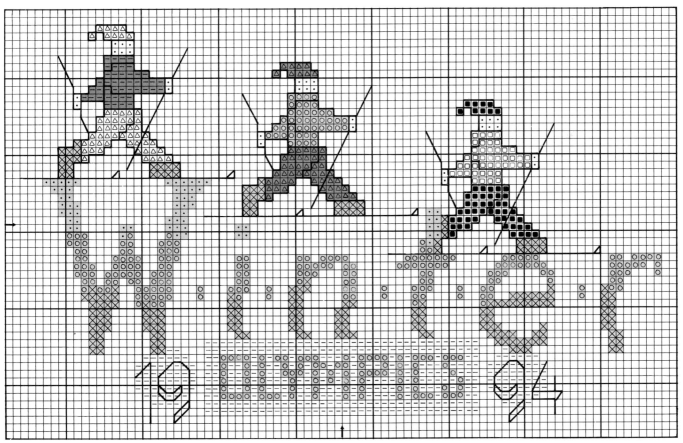

**Stitch Count: 84 x 52**

# 1-2-3-Ski!

**SAMPLE**
Stitched with Waste Canvas 10 on a purchased sweatshirt, the finished design size is 8⅜" x 5¼". The canvas was cut 10" x 7". See page 137 for working with waste canvas.

**FABRICS**

| FABRICS | DESIGN SIZES |
|---------|--------------|
| Aida 11 | 7⅝" x 4¾" |
| Aida 14 | 6" x 3¾" |
| Aida 18 | 4⅝" x 2⅞" |
| Hardanger 22 | 3⅞" x 2⅜" |

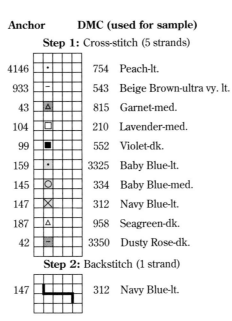

| Anchor | | DMC (used for sample) | |
|--------|--|------|------|

**Step 1:** Cross-stitch (5 strands)

| Anchor | Symbol | DMC | Name |
|--------|--------|-----|------|
| 4146 | · | 754 | Peach-lt. |
| 933 | − | 543 | Beige Brown-ultra vy. lt. |
| 43 | ▲ | 815 | Garnet-med. |
| 104 | □ | 210 | Lavender-med. |
| 99 | ■ | 552 | Violet-dk. |
| 159 | · | 3325 | Baby Blue-lt. |
| 145 | ○ | 334 | Baby Blue-med. |
| 147 | ✕ | 312 | Navy Blue-lt. |
| 187 | △ | 958 | Seagreen-dk. |
| 42 | − | 3350 | Dusty Rose-dk. |

**Step 2:** Backstitch (1 strand)

| 147 | | 312 | Navy Blue-lt. |
|-----|--|-----|---------------|

**Stitches to Go On**
Break the winter chill by donning a red or black thermal shirt stitched with this icy blue design. For the athlete, work a row of skiers across the top border of a cozy flannel sheet.

# World Marriage Day

*Express your admiration for a special couple by honoring their marriage with a joyful remembrance. Here, happy twosomes move hand in hand, enchanting their animal friends.*

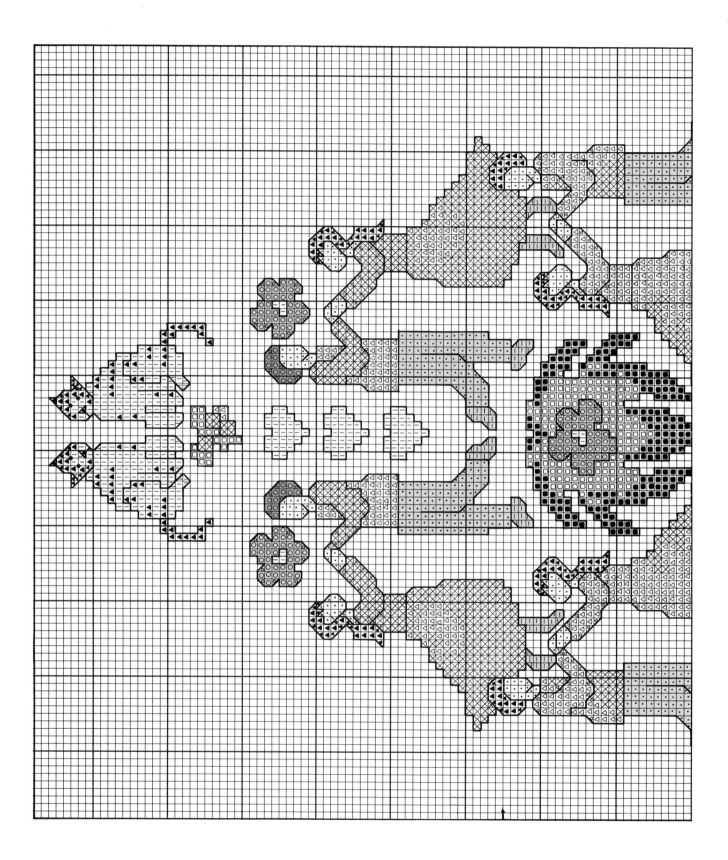

**Stitch Count: 99 x 122**

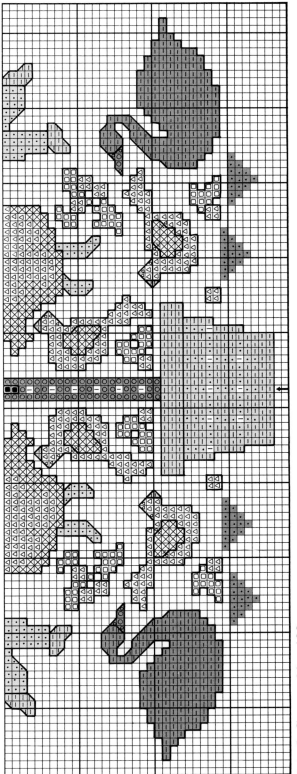

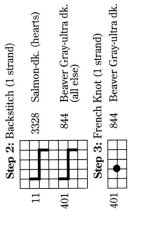

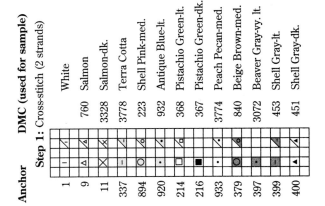

| | | Anchor | DMC (used for sample) |
|---|---|---|---|

**Step 1:** Cross-stitch (2 strands)

| | | Anchor | DMC | |
|---|---|---|---|---|
| | | 1 | | White |
| △ | | 9 | 760 | Salmon |
| ✕ | | 11 | 3328 | Salmon-dk. |
| ╱ | | 337 | | Terra Cotta |
| ○ | | 894 | 3778 | Shell Pink-med. |
| • | | 920 | 223 | Antique Blue-lt. |
| ◹ | □ | 214 | 932 | Pistachio Green-lt. |
| | ■ | 216 | 368 | Pistachio Green-dk. |
| • | • | 933 | 367 | Peach Pecan-med. |
| ◎ | ○ | 379 | 3774 | Beige Brown-med. |
| • | • | 397 | 840 | Beaver Gray-vy. lt. |
| ◥ | | 399 | 3072 | Shell Gray-lt. |
| ◀ | ◀ | 400 | 453 | Shell Gray-dk. |
| | | | 451 | |

**Step 2:** Backstitch (1 strand)

| | | |
|---|---|---|
| | 11 | 3328 Salmon-dk. (hearts) |
| | 401 | 844 Beaver Gray-ultra dk. (all else) |

**Step 3:** French Knot (1 strand)

| | | |
|---|---|---|
| ● | 401 | 844 Beaver Gray-ultra dk. |

# Dance of Love

**SAMPLE**
Stitched on carnation pink damask Aida 14 over 1 thread, the finished design size is 7⅛" x 8¾". The fabric was cut 14" x 15". See page 140 for framing ideas.

**FABRICS**      **DESIGN SIZES**
Aida 11      9" x 11⅛"
Aida 18      5½" x 6¾"
Hardanger 22      4½" x 5½"

# Valentine's Day

*Modern valentine greetings
originated in Victorian England, where
sweethearts exchanged beautifully decorated cards.
This elegant needlework-and-paper
project is reminiscent of those elaborate sentiments.
Over the years it will become a treasure
for your special valentine.*

## Hearts and Flowers

**SAMPLE for Design 1**
Stitched on white Perforated Paper 14, the finished design size is 4⅞" x 4⅝". The paper was cut 6" x 6". Begin stitching center of motif in center of paper. See page 137 for working with perforated paper and page 140 for framing ideas.

| FABRICS | DESIGN SIZES |
|---|---|
| Aida 11 | 6¼" x 5¾" |
| Aida 14 | 4⅞" x 4⅝" |
| Aida 18 | 3⅞" x 3½" |
| Hardanger 22 | 3⅛" x 2⅞" |

**SAMPLE for Design 2**
Stitched on white Perforated Paper 14, the finished design size is 3¼" x 3". The paper was cut 5" x 5". Begin stitching center of motif in center of paper.

| FABRICS | DESIGN SIZES |
|---|---|
| Aida 11 | 4⅛" x 3⅞" |
| Aida 14 | 3¼" x 3" |
| Aida 18 | 2½" x 2⅜" |
| Hardanger 22 | 2⅛" x 1⅞" |

**Stitch Count: 69 x 64 (Design 1)**

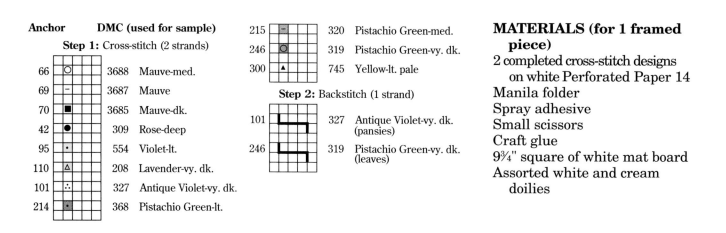

| Anchor | | DMC (used for sample) |
|---|---|---|
| **Step 1: Cross-stitch (2 strands)** | | |
| 66 | ○ | 3688 Mauve-med. |
| 69 | – | 3687 Mauve |
| 70 | ■ | 3685 Mauve-dk. |
| 42 | ● | 309 Rose-deep |
| 95 | · | 554 Violet-lt. |
| 110 | △ | 208 Lavender-vy. dk. |
| 101 | ∴ | 327 Antique Violet-vy. dk. |
| 214 | ◦ | 368 Pistachio Green-lt. |

| | | |
|---|---|---|
| 215 | – | 320 Pistachio Green-med. |
| 246 | ◯ | 319 Pistachio Green-vy. dk. |
| 300 | ▲ | 745 Yellow-lt. pale |
| **Step 2: Backstitch (1 strand)** | | |
| 101 | | 327 Antique Violet-vy. dk. (pansies) |
| 246 | | 319 Pistachio Green-vy. dk. (leaves) |

**MATERIALS (for 1 framed piece)**
2 completed cross-stitch designs
 on white Perforated Paper 14
Manila folder
Spray adhesive
Small scissors
Craft glue
9¾" square of white mat board
Assorted white and cream
 doilies

**Stitch Count: 46 x 42 (Design 2)**

## DIRECTIONS

**1.** Open folder and place on flat surface. Lightly coat 1 side with spray adhesive. Press design pieces onto folder and let dry.

**2.** Cut out each design 1 hole outside stitched area, taking care not to cut into any hole holding a stitch.

**3.** From remaining folder, cut ½" x 7" strip and fold as indicated in Diagram. Glue tab to inside of opposite end of strip. Center and glue 1 long edge to bottom of Design 2.

**4.** Glue doilies randomly to cover mat board, overlapping edges of doilies and trimming even with edges of board.

**5.** Center and glue Design 1 to prepared mat board. Measure and lightly mark 2½" down from bottom of center purple pansy. Glue base of Design 2 to mat board at this mark. Design 2 will slightly overlap Design 1, creating a 3-dimensional effect.

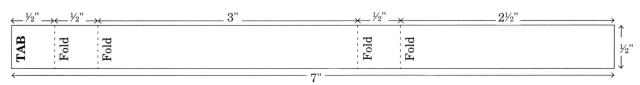

**Diagram**

# St. Patrick's Day

*A New York City tradition since 1762, the
St. Patrick's Day Parade draws more than a million
Irish and Irish-for-a-day to Fifth Avenue. Add a bit o' the
green with this simple shamrock, shown here on a shirt
pocket and worked into festive button covers.*

# Shamrock Shirt

## SAMPLE
Stitched with Waste Canvas 14 on pocket of purchased shirt, the finished design size is 4⅝" x 1⅞". The canvas was cut 6" x 3". See page 137 for working with waste canvas and page 142 for flower thread.

| FABRICS | DESIGN SIZES |
|---------|--------------|
| Aida 11 | 5⅞" x 2½" |
| Aida 14 | 4⅝" x 1⅞" |
| Aida 18 | 3⅝" x 1½" |
| Hardanger 22 | 3" x 1¼" |

## MATERIALS
Purchased white shirt with pocket; matching thread
Contrasting thread
Scrap of waste canvas
DMC Flower Thread #2958
Liquid ravel preventer

**DMC Flower Thread**
**(used for sample)**
**Step 1:** Cross-stitch (1 strand)

| | | | | | |
|---|---|---|---|---|---|
| O | | | | | 2958 Jade-vy. dk. |

## DIRECTIONS
**1.** Remove pocket and loose threads from pocket area of shirt. Baste over fold lines with contrasting thread and press seams open. Apply liquid ravel preventer to raw edges; let dry.

**2.** Center waste canvas on design area, 1¼" from top of pocket. Baste in place. Center and begin stitching ¼" below top of waste canvas.

**3.** Remove waste canvas; let pocket dry. Turn pocket top edge under twice to basting line; press and hem. Turn pocket side and bottom edges under to basting line and press. Remove basting thread and machine-stitch pocket to shirt front in original position.

### Stitches to Go On
Spread the luck of the Irish by edging a tea towel with shamrocks or by decorating a set of cocktail napkins with a single shamrock in each corner. Embellish a baby's bib for a lucky little leprechaun.

# Shamrock Button Covers

## SAMPLE
Stitched on antique green Hardanger 22 over 1 thread, the finished design size is ⅝" x ⅝" for each. The fabric was cut into a 2"-diameter circle for each. Stitch 5.

## MATERIALS
5 completed cross-stitch designs on antique green Hardanger 22
5 (1⅛") covered button forms
5 button covers
Hot-glue gun and glue sticks

## DIRECTIONS
*Note:* Finished button covers are shown actual size.

**1.** Remove shank from 1 covered button form.

**2.** With design centered, follow manufacturer's instructions to cover button form.

**3.** Center and glue completed covered button form to button cover. Let dry. Repeat for remaining button covers.

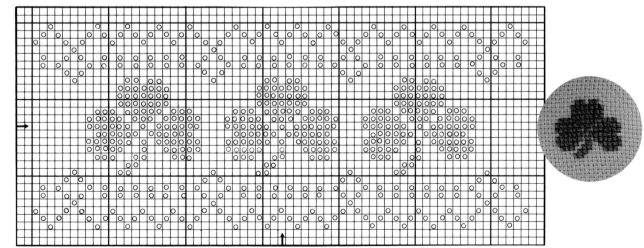

**Stitch Count: 65 x 27 (for complete design)**
**15 x 13 (for 1 shamrock)**

## MARCH 21

# *First Day of*
# *Spring*

*Spring is a time of new beginnings.*
*The flowers of the season, like these hollyhocks,*
*renew us after winter and urge us to look forward to the*
*months ahead. Celebrate each season by completing*
*our Four Seasons cross-stitch collection.*

**Stitch Count: 128 x 103**

# Hollyhocks

## SAMPLE

Stitched on white Belfast Linen 32 over 2 threads, the finished design size is 8" x 6½". The fabric was cut 14" x 13".

| FABRICS | DESIGN SIZES |
|---|---|
| Aida 11 | 11⅝" x 9⅜" |
| Aida 14 | 9⅛" x 7⅜" |
| Aida 18 | 7⅛" x 5¾" |
| Hardanger 22 | 5⅞" x 4⅝" |

| Anchor | | | DMC | (used for sample) |
|---|---|---|---|---|

**Step 1:** Cross-stitch (2 strands)

| Anchor | | | DMC | |
|---|---|---|---|---|
| 1 | | | | White |
| 297 | | | 743 | Yellow-med. |
| 4146 | | | 754 | Peach-lt. |
| 26 | | | 3708 | Melon-lt. |
| 28 | | | 3706 | Melon-med. |
| 50 | | | 605 | Cranberry-vy. lt. |
| 76 | | | 603 | Cranberry |
| 77 | | | 602 | Cranberry-med. |
| 95 | | | 554 | Violet-lt. |
| 117 | | | 3747 | Blue Violet-vy. lt. |
| 118 | | | 340 | Blue Violet-med. |
| 149 | | | 311 | Navy Blue-med. |
| 264 | | | 772 | Pine Green-lt. |
| 206 | | | 955 | Nile Green-lt. |
| 203 | | | 954 | Nile Green |
| 204 | | | 912 | Emerald Green-lt. |
| 228 | | | 910 | Emerald Green-dk. |
| 347 | | | 402 | Mahogany-vy. lt. |

**Step 2:** Backstitch (1 strand)

| 149 | | 311 | Navy Blue-med. |
|---|---|---|---|

# Easter

*This irresistible bunny blooms
with the colors of a spring bouquet—
let it hop into someone's basket this Easter.
The versatile cross-stitch motifs decorating this
cuddly cottontail can also be used on a
variety of other projects; see the box
on page 38 for ideas.*

# Pink Blossom Bunny

**SAMPLE**
Stitched on ash rose and white Annabelle 28 over 2 threads, the finished design sizes for 1 motif are: 1⅜" x 1⅜" for Flowers, 1⅛" x 1⅛" for Cherries and Lattice, and 1⅝" x 1⅜" for Rose. See Steps 1 and 2 of Directions before stitching and cutting fabrics.

**Flowers** (head back, forehead, head sides, nose sides)

| FABRICS | DESIGN SIZES |
|---|---|
| Aida 11 | 1⅞" x 1⅞" |
| Aida 14 | 1⅜" x 1⅜" |
| Aida 18 | 1⅛" x 1⅛" |
| Hardanger 22 | ⅞" x ⅞" |

**Cherries** (front legs, inner hind legs, outer hind legs)

| FABRICS | DESIGN SIZES |
|---|---|
| Aida 11 | 1½" x 1½" |
| Aida 14 | 1⅛" x 1⅛" |
| Aida 18 | ⅞" x ⅞" |
| Hardanger 22 | ¾" x ¾" |

**Lattice** (ears, stomach)

| FABRICS | DESIGN SIZES |
|---|---|
| Aida 11 | 1½" x 1½" |
| Aida 14 | 1⅛" x 1⅛" |
| Aida 18 | ⅞" x ⅞" |
| Hardanger 22 | ¾" x ¾" |

**Rose** (tail)

| FABRICS | DESIGN SIZES |
|---|---|
| Aida 11 | 2" x 1¾" |
| Aida 14 | 1⅝" x 1⅜" |
| Aida 18 | 1¼" x 1" |
| Hardanger 22 | 1" x ⅞" |

**MATERIALS**
¼ yard of unstitched ash rose Annabelle 28; matching thread
⅛ yard of unstitched white Annabelle 28; matching thread
⅜ yard of fusible knit interfacing
1 skein of #5 DMC Pearl Cotton 816
2 (½") purple shank buttons
⅞ yard each of 1"-wide light green, light pink, and medium pink sheer ribbon
Darning needle
Stuffing
Tracing paper
Dressmaker's pen

## DIRECTIONS

The patterns begin on page 40 and include ¼" seam allowances.

**1.** Transfer patterns to tracing paper and cut out. Using dressmaker's pen, transfer the following patterns to ash rose Annabelle: head back, forehead, head sides, nose sides, front legs, body fronts, body backs, inner hind legs, outer hind legs, and bottom; *do not cut out.* Transfer the following patterns to white Annabelle: ears and stomach; *do not cut out.* For tail, draw a 5¾"-diameter circle on white Annabelle; *do not cut out.*

Referring to sample information, cross-stitch designs on bunny pieces, beginning in the center of each piece and repeating motif to fill patterns. For ears, stitch design on 1 ear and 1 reversed ear piece. For tail, center and stitch 1 rose motif.

**2.** Fuse interfacing to wrong side of fabrics, following manufacturer's directions. Cut out pieces.

**3.** To make ears, with right sides facing and raw edges aligned, stitch 1 ear design piece to 1 unstitched ear, leaving straight edge open. Clip curves, turn, and press. Handling both layers as 1, fold a 1" pleat in open end (see Diagram 1) with pleat folded toward back of ear; baste. Repeat for other ear.

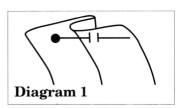

**Diagram 1**

**4.** To make head front, stitch darts in forehead and head side pieces. With right sides facing and raw edges aligned, stitch 1 nose side piece to 1 head side piece (see patterns). Repeat for other nose and head side pieces.

**5.** With right sides facing, raw edges aligned, and back of ears toward back of forehead, baste 1 ear to each side of forehead (see pattern). With right sides facing and raw edges aligned, stitch forehead to each head/nose side, stitching across ears twice and pivoting at dot at tip of forehead (see patterns).

**6.** To finish head, stitch head front to head back, leaving center front seam and neck open (see patterns).

**7.** To make body, with right sides facing and raw edges aligned, stitch 2 front leg pieces together, leaving open where indicated (see pattern). Clip curves and turn. Repeat for other front leg.

With paw down and raw edges aligned, stitch 1 front leg to right side of each body back (see patterns). With right sides facing and raw edges aligned, stitch 1 body back to each body front along side seam. With right sides facing and raw edges aligned, stitch body

**Stitches to Go On**
For a great gift, stitch the rose atop a potpourri jar lid or trim a checked tea towel with the cherry motif. Cover a jewelry box with the lattice design. The flowers can bloom on the corner of a linen hankie.

together along center back seam; then stitch center front seam from bottom edge to dot (see pattern), taking care not to catch front legs in seam.

**8.** To make hind legs, stitch darts in 1 outer hind leg (see pattern). With right sides facing and dot on 1 inner hind leg matching dot on 1 outer hind leg, stitch from dot to toe following arrows, reinforcing with additional stitching where indicated (see patterns). Repeat for other hind leg.

**9.** With raw edges aligned and top center dart and body side seam matching, stitch 1 hind leg to right side of body, beginning at bottom edge of body back and continuing to bottom edge of body front. Repeat for other hind leg.

**10.** Run gathering threads where indicated on body front and inner hind legs (see patterns). Pull to gather threads tightly; secure.

**11.** With right sides facing, sew bottom to body, matching center front and center back seams to marks on bottom (see pattern).

**12.** With right sides facing, stitch head to body, matching side seams. Stitch center front seam from nose to 1" below neck. Trim corners and clip curves. Turn bunny through opening in body front.

**13.** Stuff front legs; slipstitch openings closed. Stuff bunny firmly; slipstitch opening closed.

**14.** Turn under edge of stomach design piece ¼" to wrong side; baste. Referring to photo, center stomach on bunny and pin. Slipstitch in place.

## Cherries

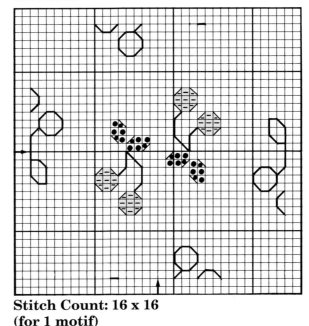

**Stitch Count: 16 x 16
(for 1 motif)**

**15.** Using 6 strands of pearl cotton, satin-stitch nose at point of forehead/nose seam (see Diagram 2). Without cutting thread, make 2 (¼"-long) straightstitches along center front seam. For eyes, using darning needle and 4 strands of thread, attach 1 button ¼" from head side/forehead seam. Without cutting thread, push needle through to opposite side of head and then through second button (see Diagram 2). Sew back and forth between buttons, pulling thread tightly to indent head. Secure thread.

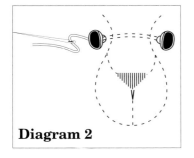

**Diagram 2**

**16.** To make tail, run gathering threads around edge of tail; pull to gather threads loosely. Stuff tail firmly. Pull to gather threads tightly; secure. With gathered edge tucked under, secure tail to base of center back seam, slipstitching completely around tail.

**17.** Handling all ribbons as 1, tie into a bow around bunny's neck. Trim ribbons to desired length; notch ends.

## Rose

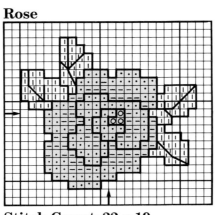

**Stitch Count: 22 x 19
(for 1 motif)**

## Flowers

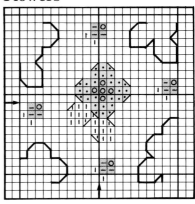

**Stitch Count: 20 x 20
(for 1 motif)**

## Lattice

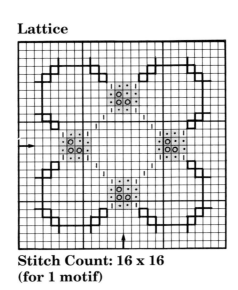

**Stitch Count: 16 x 16
(for 1 motif)**

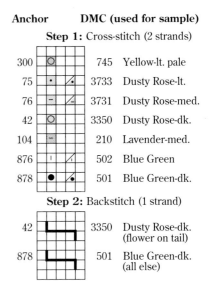

| Anchor | | | DMC | (used for sample) |
|---|---|---|---|---|

**Step 1:** Cross-stitch (2 strands)

| 300 | ○ | | 745 | Yellow-lt. pale |
| 75 | · | ╱ | 3733 | Dusty Rose-lt. |
| 76 | – | ╱ | 3731 | Dusty Rose-med. |
| 42 | ○ | | 3350 | Dusty Rose-dk. |
| 104 | | | 210 | Lavender-med. |
| 876 | I | ╱ | 502 | Blue Green |
| 878 | ● | ╱ | 501 | Blue Green-dk. |

**Step 2:** Backstitch (1 strand)

| 42 | | | 3350 | Dusty Rose-dk. (flower on tail) |
| 878 | | | 501 | Blue Green-dk. (all else) |

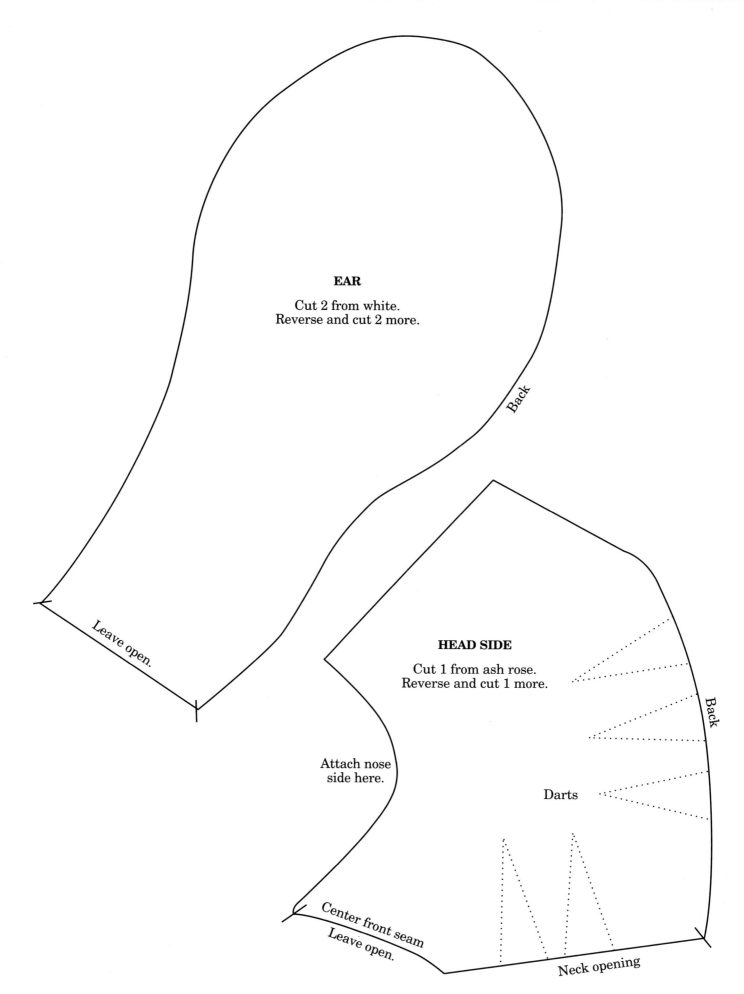

**EAR**

Cut 2 from white.
Reverse and cut 2 more.

Back

Leave open.

**HEAD SIDE**

Cut 1 from ash rose.
Reverse and cut 1 more.

Back

Attach nose
side here.

Darts

Center front seam
Leave open.

Neck opening

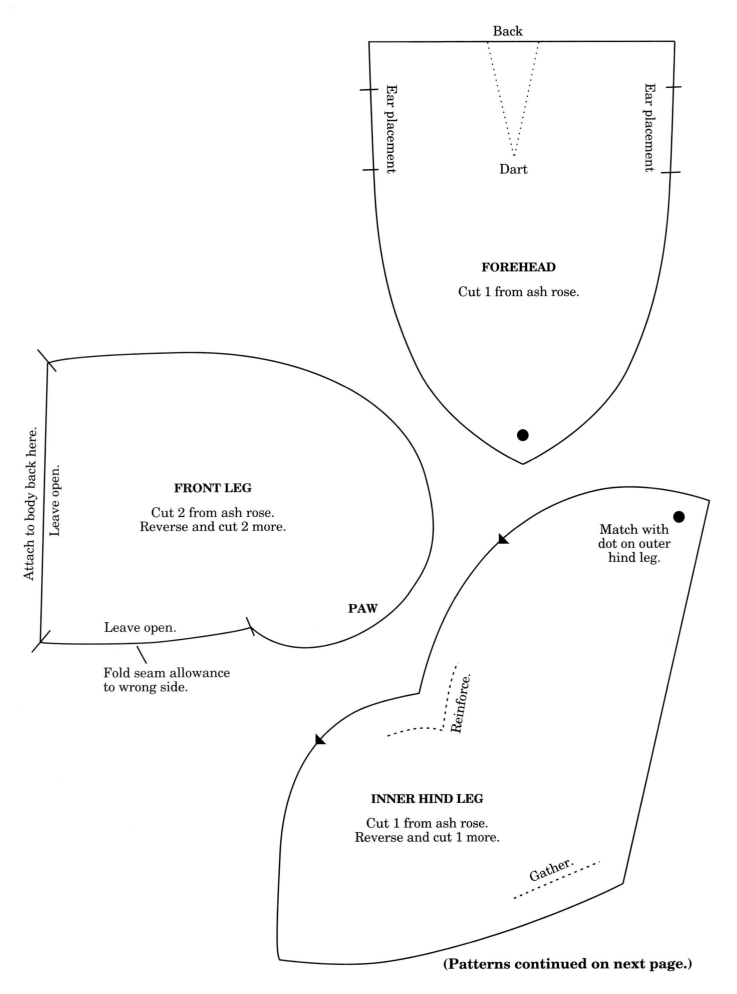

Back

Ear placement

Ear placement

Dart

**FOREHEAD**

Cut 1 from ash rose.

Attach to body back here.

Leave open.

**FRONT LEG**

Cut 2 from ash rose.
Reverse and cut 2 more.

Leave open.

Fold seam allowance
to wrong side.

**PAW**

Match with
dot on outer
hind leg.

Reinforce.

**INNER HIND LEG**

Cut 1 from ash rose.
Reverse and cut 1 more.

Gather.

**(Patterns continued on next page.)**

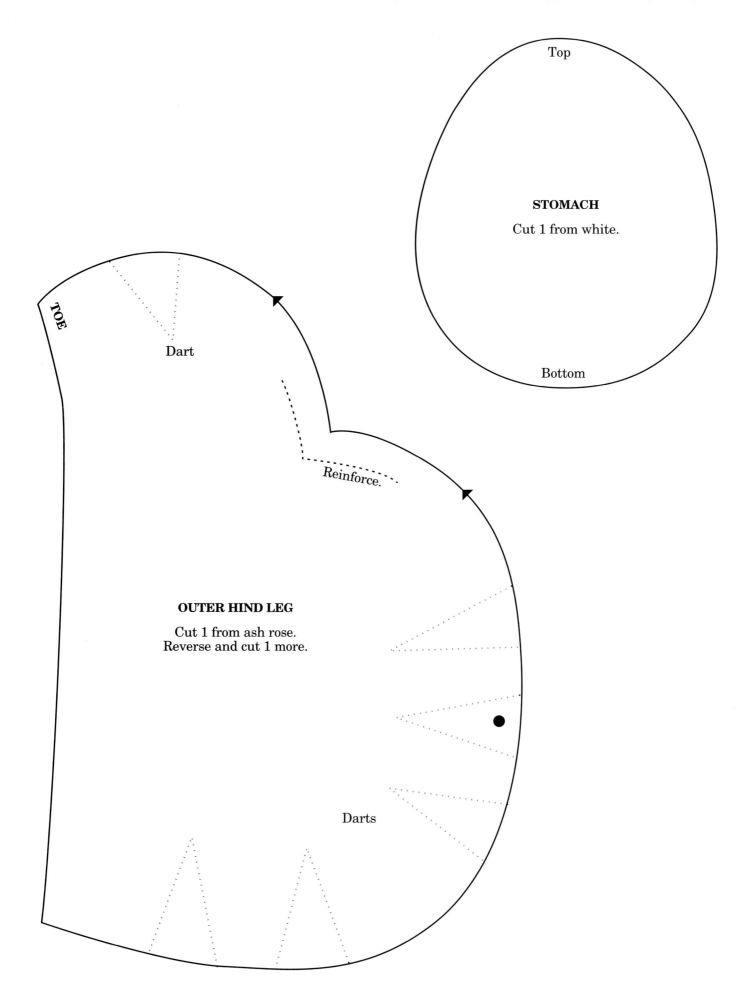

**STOMACH**

Cut 1 from white.

Top

Bottom

TOE

Dart

Reinforce.

**OUTER HIND LEG**

Cut 1 from ash rose.
Reverse and cut 1 more.

Darts

42

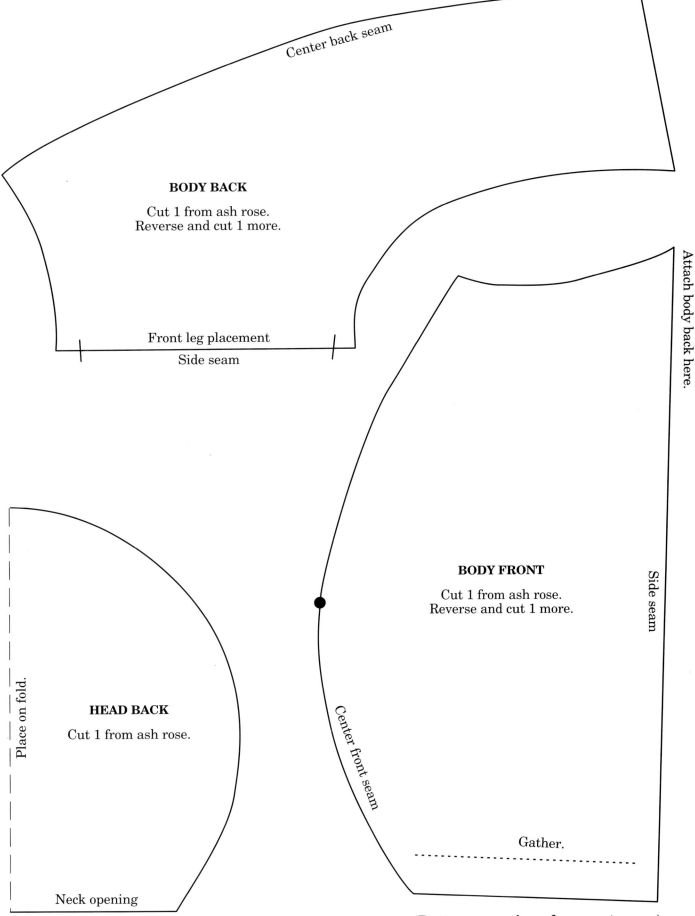

Center back seam

**BODY BACK**

Cut 1 from ash rose.
Reverse and cut 1 more.

Front leg placement

Side seam

Attach body back here.

**BODY FRONT**

Cut 1 from ash rose.
Reverse and cut 1 more.

Side seam

Place on fold.

**HEAD BACK**

Cut 1 from ash rose.

Center front seam

Gather.

Neck opening

**(Patterns continued on next page.)**

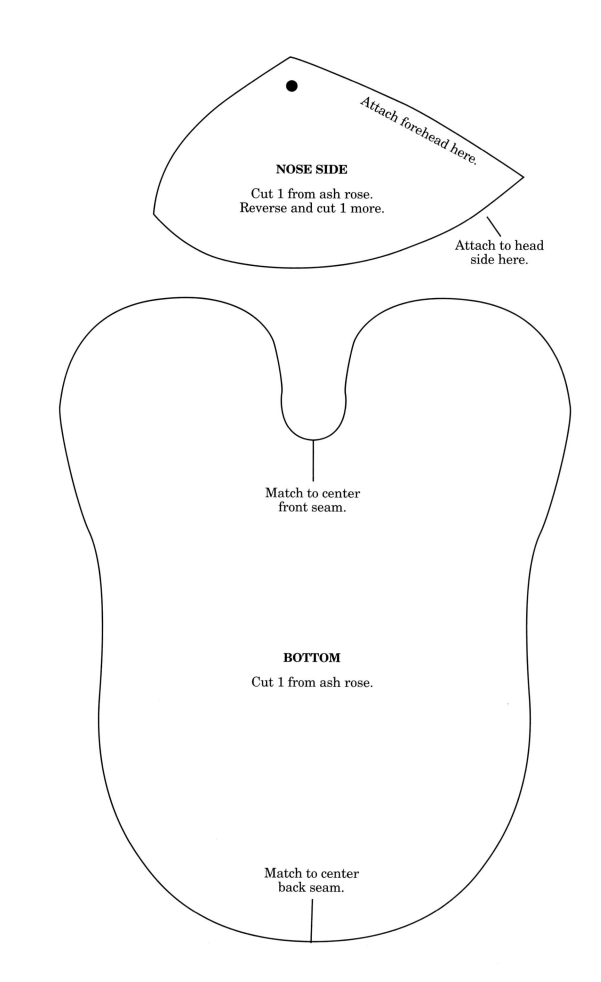

Attach forehead here.

**NOSE SIDE**

Cut 1 from ash rose.
Reverse and cut 1 more.

Attach to head
side here.

Match to center
front seam.

**BOTTOM**

Cut 1 from ash rose.

Match to center
back seam.

# APRIL 23
## *St. George's Day*

*According to the tale, in the year 303
St. George slew the dragon to save a young maiden.
That brave act of chivalry is what the patron saint of
England is best remembered for today.*

46

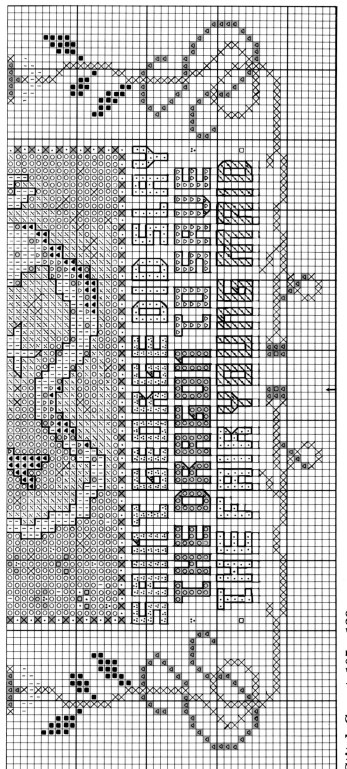

**Stitch Count: 105 x 139**

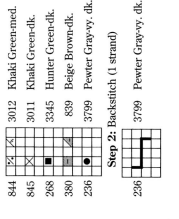

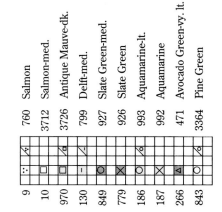

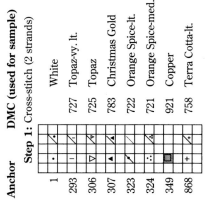

# Dragon Slayer

**SAMPLE**
Stitched on pewter Murano 30 over 2 threads, the finished design size is 7" x 9¼". The fabric was cut 13" x 15".

| FABRICS | DESIGN SIZES |
|---|---|
| Aida 11 | 9½" x 12⅝" |
| Aida 14 | 7½" x 9⅞" |
| Aida 18 | 5⅞" x 7¾" |
| Hardanger 22 | 4¾" x 6⅜" |

| Anchor | | DMC (used for sample) | |
|---|---|---|---|
| | | **Step 1:** Cross-stitch (2 strands) | |
| 1 | · | | White |
| 293 | – | 727 | Topaz-vy. lt. |
| 306 | ▽ | 725 | Topaz |
| 307 | ▲ | 783 | Christmas Gold |
| 323 | ✓ | 722 | Orange Spice-lt. |
| 324 | ∷ | 721 | Orange Spice-med. |
| 349 | ■ | 921 | Copper |
| 868 | + | 758 | Terra Cotta-lt. |
| 9 | ∷ | 760 | Salmon |
| 10 | □ | 3712 | Salmon-med. |
| 970 | ◢ | 3726 | Antique Mauve-dk. |
| 130 | – | 799 | Delft-med. |
| 849 | ◯ | 927 | Slate Green-med. |
| 779 | ⊠ | 926 | Slate Green |
| 186 | ◯ | 993 | Aquamarine-lt. |
| 187 | ◢ | 992 | Aquamarine |
| 266 | ◣ | 471 | Avocado Green-vy. lt. |
| 843 | ◯ | 3364 | Pine Green |
| 844 | ▨ | 3012 | Khaki Green-med. |
| 845 | ⊠ | 3011 | Khaki Green-dk. |
| 268 | ■ | 3345 | Hunter Green-dk. |
| 380 | ◣ | 839 | Beige Brown-dk. |
| 236 | ● | 3799 | Pewter Gray-vy. dk. |
| | | **Step 2:** Backstitch (1 strand) | |
| 236 | | 3799 | Pewter Gray-vy. dk. |

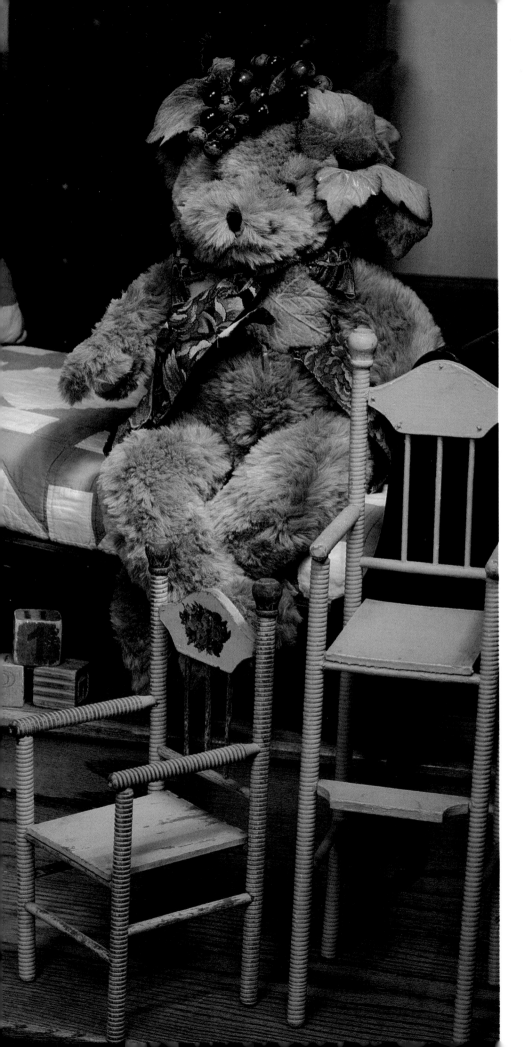

# Better Sleep Month

*This snoozing bruin may make your little ones actually look forward to climbing into bed. A cozy blanket, a bedtime story, and a favorite bear will guarantee a good night's sleep for all!*

# Pleasant Dreams

## SAMPLE

Stitched on white Aida 14 over 1 thread, the finished design size is 10⅜" x 15⅜". The fabric was cut 17" x 22".

| FABRICS | DESIGN SIZES |
|---|---|
| Aida 11 | 13⅛" x 19⅝" |
| Aida 18 | 8⅛" x 11⅞" |
| Hardanger 22 | 6⅝" x 9¾" |

| Anchor | | | DMC | (used for sample) |
|---|---|---|---|---|

**Step 1: Cross-stitch (2 strands)**

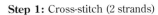

| Anchor | | | DMC | |
|---|---|---|---|---|
| 1 | · | ⁄ | | White |
| 300 | ▣ | · | 745 | Yellow-lt. pale |
| 306 | ⨉ | ⧄ | 725 | Topaz |
| 868 | ⦀ | ⁄ | 758 | Terra Cotta-lt. |
| 329 | △ | ◹ | 3340 | Apricot-med. |
| 11 | ⫶ | ◸ | 350 | Coral-med. |
| 75 | + | ◹ | 604 | Cranberry-lt. |
| 76 | ☐ | ◪ | 603 | Cranberry |
| 869 | – | | 3743 | Antique Violet-vy. lt. |
| 108 | + | ◹ | 211 | Lavender-lt. |
| 105 | ⫶ | ◹ | 209 | Lavender-dk. |
| 975 | ⁄ | ◹ | 3753 | Antique Blue-vy. lt. |
| 128 | · | ◹ | 800 | Delft-pale |
| 161 | ○ | ◶ | 826 | Blue-med. |
| 940 | ⨉ | ◹ | 792 | Cornflower Blue-dk. |
| 928 | ▽ | ◹ | 598 | Turquoise-lt. |

**Color code continued on page 52.**

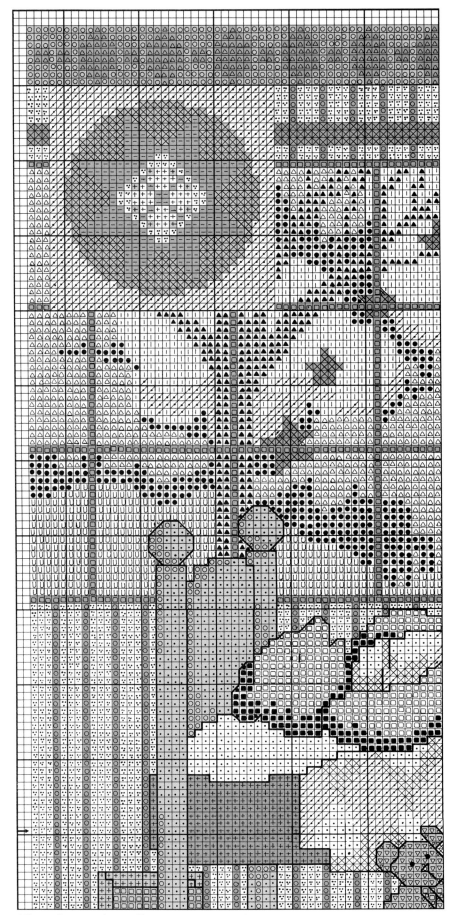

**(Graph continued on next page.)**

| 167 | 597 | Turquoise |
| 203 | 954 | Nile Green |
| 205 | 911 | Emerald Green-med. |
| 347 | 402 | Mahogany-vy. lt. |
| 338 | 3776 | Mahogany-lt. |
| 376 | 842 | Beige Brown-vy. lt. |
| 380 | 839 | Beige Brown-dk. |
| 397 | 453 | Shell Gray-lt. |
| 236 | 3799 | Pewter Gray-vy. dk. |
| 1 | | White (1 strand) |
| 397 | 453 | Shell Gray-lt. (1 strand) |
| 869 | 3743 | Antique Violet-vy. lt. (1 strand) |
| 397 | 453 | Shell Gray-lt. (1 strand) |
| 203 | 954 | Nile Green (1 strand) |
| 397 | 453 | Shell Gray-lt. (1 strand) |
| 378 | 841 | Beige Brown-lt. (1 strand) |
| 397 | 453 | Shell Gray-lt. (1 strand) |

**Step 2:** Backstitch (1 strand)

| 329 | 3340 | Apricot-med. (lines in toy top) |
| 940 | 792 | Cornflower Blue-dk. (alphabet) |
| 236 | 3799 | Pewter Gray-vy. dk. (all else) |

**Step 3:** French Knot (1 strand)

| 236 | 3799 | Pewter Gray-vy. dk. |

**Stitch Count: 145 x 215**

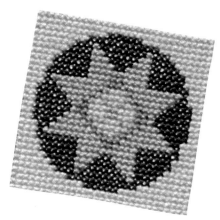

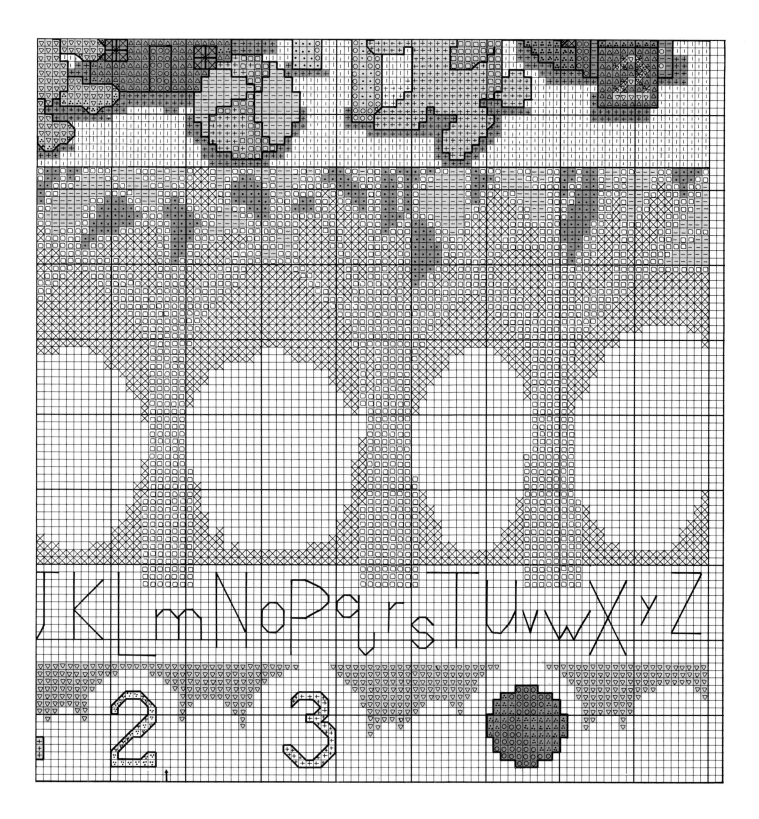

# Mother Goose Day

*For generations Mother Goose nursery rhymes have been read to eager young ears. The gleeful verses about Mary and her devoted lamb are crystallized here in cross-stitch. With its childlike palette, this piece will be a welcome addition to a little one's nursery.*

## Mary and Her Lamb

### SAMPLE

Stitched on white Belfast Linen 32 over 2 threads, the finished design size is 4⅜" x 6⅛". The fabric was cut 11" x 13".

| FABRICS | DESIGN SIZES |
|---|---|
| Aida 11 | 6⅜" x 8⅞" |
| Aida 14 | 5" x 7" |
| Aida 18 | 3⅞" x 5½" |
| Hardanger 22 | 3⅛" x 4½" |

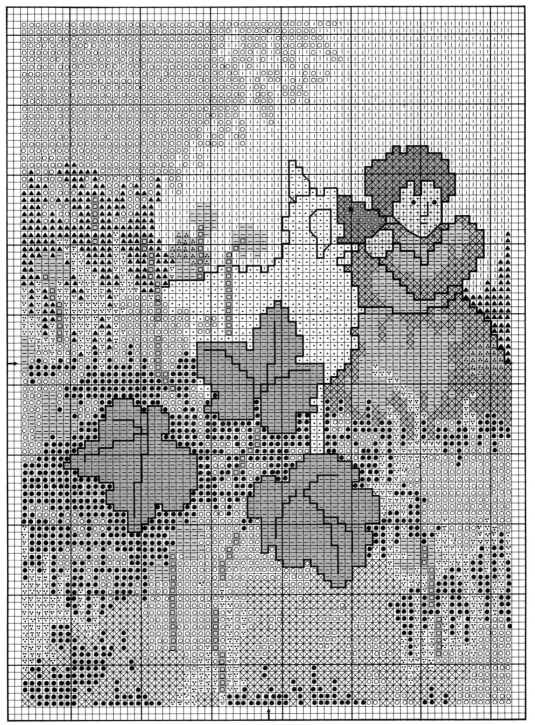

**Stitch Count: 70 x 98**

| Anchor | | DMC (used for sample) |
|---|---|---|

**Step 1:** Cross-stitch (2 strands)

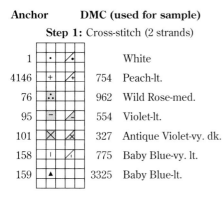

| 1 | White |
|---|---|
| 4146 | 754 Peach-lt. |
| 76 | 962 Wild Rose-med. |
| 95 | 554 Violet-lt. |
| 101 | 327 Antique Violet-vy. dk. |
| 158 | 775 Baby Blue-vy. lt. |
| 159 | 3325 Baby Blue-lt. |

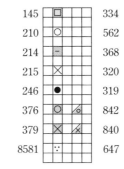

| 145 | 334 Baby Blue-med. |
|---|---|
| 210 | 562 Jade-med. |
| 214 | 368 Pistachio Green-lt. |
| 215 | 320 Pistachio Green-med. |
| 246 | 319 Pistachio Green-vy. dk. |
| 376 | 842 Beige Brown-vy. lt. |
| 379 | 840 Beige Brown-med. |
| 8581 | 647 Beaver Gray-med. |

**Step 2:** Backstitch (1 strand)

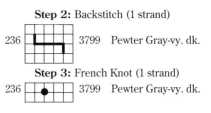

| 236 | 3799 Pewter Gray-vy. dk. |
|---|---|

**Step 3:** French Knot (1 strand)

| 236 | 3799 Pewter Gray-vy. dk. |
|---|---|

## MAY 8

# *Mother's Day*

*To thank Mother for all of the special things she does for you, pamper her with a selection of delicate package toppers for her favorite scented soaps. This unique gift will be an endearing expression of your love.*

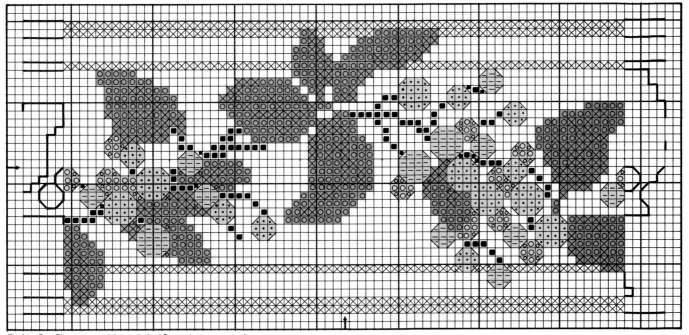

**Stitch Count: 69 x 36 (for 1 repeat)**

# Pretty Packages

**SAMPLE for Berry Border**
Stitched on natural Linen 36 over 2 threads, the finished design size for 1 repeat is 3⅞" x 2". See Steps 1 and 2 of Directions before purchasing, cutting, and stitching fabric.

| FABRICS | DESIGN SIZES |
|---|---|
| Aida 11 | 6¼" x 3¼" |
| Aida 14 | 4⅞" x 2⅝" |
| Aida 18 | 3⅞" x 2" |
| Hardanger 22 | 3⅛" x 1⅝" |

## MATERIALS
Completed cross-stitch on natural Linen 36; matching thread
Package of scented soaps

## DIRECTIONS
All seam allowances are ¼".

**1.** Before stitching design, measure around soap package and add 3½" for horizontal measurement. Add 7" to vertical measurement of motif. Cut unstitched fabric to match measurements.

**2.** Centering design vertically, begin stitching first motif 2½" from left edge of fabric. Repeat motif across fabric, leaving 1" unstitched at opposite end.

**3.** Measure and mark 1½" above and below design; trim fabric. Trim ¾" from each end.

**4.** With right sides facing and long edges aligned, stitch long edges together to make a tube. Turn. Position seam in center back and press.

**5.** Fold left end of design piece ¼" to back. Fold remaining edge ¼" to front. Wrap band snugly around soap package. Place turned-under edge on top of unstitched section on opposite edge, aligning long edges and motifs. Slipstitch together along sides and ends.

| Anchor | | DMC (used for sample) | |
|---|---|---|---|
| **Step 1:** Cross-stitch (2 strands) | | | |
| 11 | | 3328 | Salmon-dk. |
| 896 | | 3722 | Shell Pink |
| 970 | | 315 | Antique Mauve-vy. dk. |
| 871 | | 3041 | Antique Violet-med. |
| 846 | | 3051 | Green Gray-dk. |
| 862 | | 935 | Avocado Green-dk. |
| 380 | | 839 | Beige Brown-dk. |

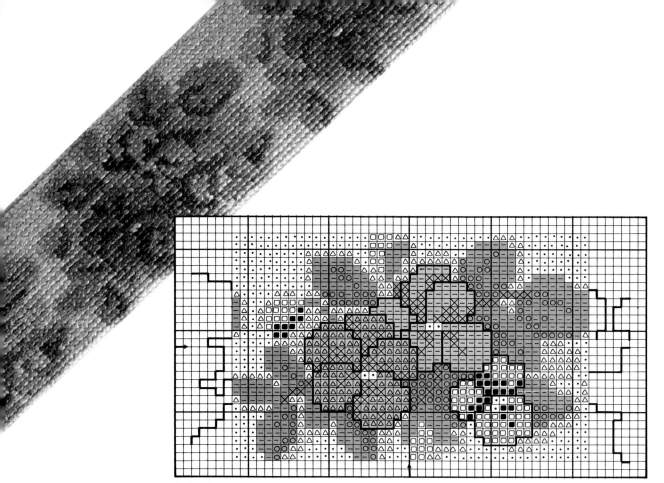

**Stitch Count: 44 x 28 (for 1 repeat)**

### SAMPLE for Pansy Border
Stitched on cream Aida 18 over 1 thread, the finished design size for 1 repeat is 2½" x 1½". See Steps 1 and 2 of Directions before purchasing, cutting, and stitching fabric.

| FABRICS | DESIGN SIZES |
|---------|--------------|
| Aida 11 | 4" x 2½" |
| Aida 14 | 3⅛" x 2" |
| Hardanger 22 | 2" x 1¼" |

### MATERIALS
Completed cross-stitch on cream Aida 18; matching thread
Package of scented soaps

### DIRECTIONS
All seam allowances are ¼".

**1.** Before stitching design, measure around soap package and add 3½" for horizontal measurement. Add 6" to vertical measurement of motif. Cut unstitched fabric to match measurements.

**2.** To complete, repeat Steps 2–5 of Berry Border.

### Stitches to Go On
These versatile designs provide many exciting possibilities–stitch either border on hand towels or turn the completed designs into a headband or picture frame. Use the round peach motif for a compact case or jewelry box top.

| Anchor | | DMC (used for sample) | |
|--------|---|-----|---|
| **Step 1:** Cross-stitch (2 strands) | | | |
| 887 | · | 3046 | Yellow Beige-med. |
| 373 | △ | 3045 | Yellow Beige-dk. |
| 896 | △ | 3722 | Shell Pink |
| 969 | – | 316 | Antique Mauve-med. |
| 970 | ✕ | 315 | Antique Mauve-vy. dk. |
| 870 | □ | 3042 | Antique Violet-lt. |
| 871 | ■ | 3041 | Antique Violet-med. |
| 859 | – | 3052 | Green Gray-med. |
| 846 | ○ | 3051 | Green Gray-dk. |
| 379 | ✕ | 840 | Beige Brown-med. |
| **Step 2:** Backstitch (1 strand) | | | |
| 970 | | 315 | Antique Mauve-vy. dk. (mauve pansies) |
| 871 | | 3041 | Antique Violet-med. (violet pansies) |

**58**

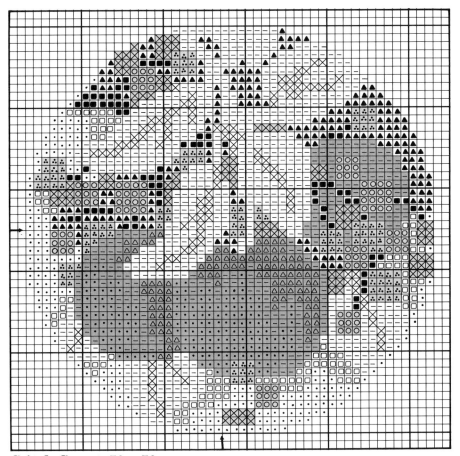

**Stitch Count: 50 x 50**

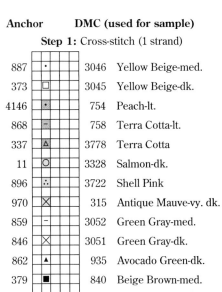

| Anchor | | DMC (used for sample) | |
|---|---|---|---|
| | | **Step 1: Cross-stitch (1 strand)** | |
| 887 | · | 3046 | Yellow Beige-med. |
| 373 | □ | 3045 | Yellow Beige-dk. |
| 4146 | · | 754 | Peach-lt. |
| 868 | − | 758 | Terra Cotta-lt. |
| 337 | △ | 3778 | Terra Cotta |
| 11 | ○ | 3328 | Salmon-dk. |
| 896 | ⁚ | 3722 | Shell Pink |
| 970 | ✕ | 315 | Antique Mauve-vy. dk. |
| 859 | − | 3052 | Green Gray-med. |
| 846 | ✕ | 3051 | Green Gray-dk. |
| 862 | ▲ | 935 | Avocado Green-dk. |
| 379 | ■ | 840 | Beige Brown-med. |

### SAMPLE for Peach Motif

Stitched on raw linen Dublin Linen 25 over 1 thread, the finished design size is 2" x 2". The fabric was cut 8" x 8". Begin stitching in center of fabric.

| FABRIC | DESIGN SIZES |
|---|---|
| Aida 11 | 4½" x 4½" |
| Aida 14 | 3⅝" x 3⅝" |
| Aida 18 | 2¾" x 2¾" |
| Hardanger 22 | 2¼" x 2¼" |

### MATERIALS

Completed cross-stitch on raw linen Dublin Linen 25; matching thread
Scrap of mat board or heavy cardboard
Scrap of polyester batting
Hot-glue gun and glue sticks
Round, decoratively wrapped scented soap

### DIRECTIONS

**1.** With design centered, trim design piece to 3½" square.

**2.** From mat board, cut 2½"-diameter circle. Using mat board circle as pattern, cut batting. Glue batting to 1 side of mat board.

**3.** Center design piece on batting. Trim design piece ½" outside of circle. Keeping fabric taut, fold over mat board to back and glue in place.

**4.** Glue design to center front of soap.

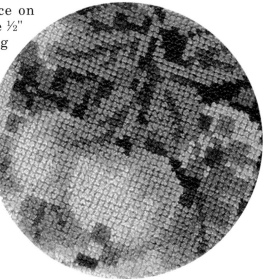

**59**

# National Rose Month

*The rose, cherished for its beauty and fragrance, is the national flower of the United States. More than one billion fresh-cut stems are sold every year. Stitch these everlasting blooms and add a floral essence to your home.*

**Stitch Count: 120 x 140**

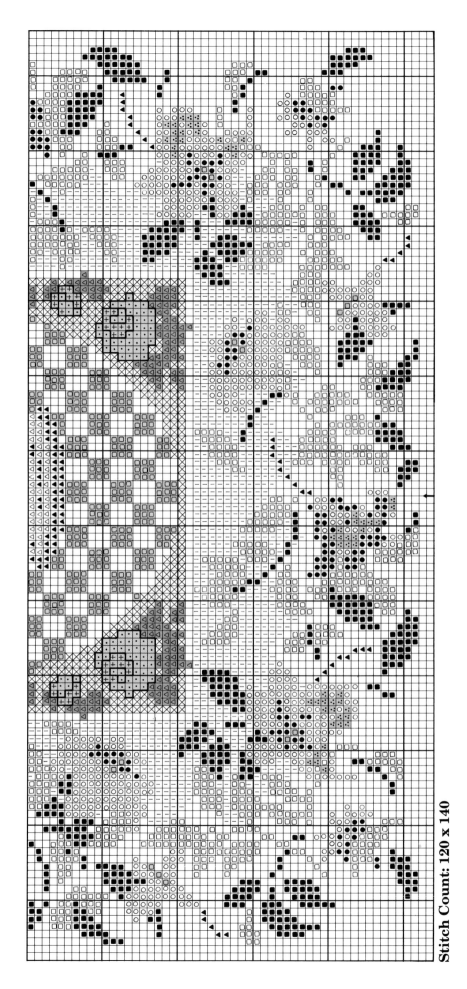
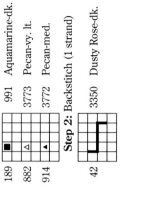
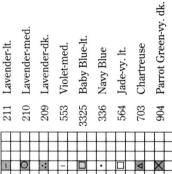
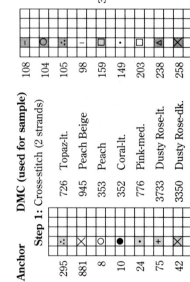

| Anchor | | DMC (used for sample) | |
|---|---|---|---|
| | | Step 1: Cross-stitch (2 strands) | |
| 295 | ∴ | 726 | Topaz-lt. |
| 881 | ☒ | 945 | Peach Beige |
| 8 | ○ | 353 | Peach |
| 10 | ● | 352 | Coral-lt. |
| 24 | | 776 | Pink-med. |
| 75 | + | 3733 | Dusty Rose-lt. |
| 42 | ☒ | 3350 | Dusty Rose-dk. |

| | | | |
|---|---|---|---|
| 108 | – | 211 | Lavender-lt. |
| 104 | ○ | 210 | Lavender-med. |
| 105 | ∴ | 209 | Lavender-dk. |
| 98 | – | 553 | Violet-med. |
| 159 | ☐ | 3325 | Baby Blue-lt. |
| 149 | · | 336 | Navy Blue |
| 203 | ☐ | 564 | Jade-vy. lt. |
| 238 | ◤ | 703 | Chartreuse |
| 258 | ☒ | 904 | Parrot Green-vy. dk. |

| | | | |
|---|---|---|---|
| 189 | ■ | 991 | Aquamarine-dk. |
| 882 | ◁ | 3773 | Pecan-lt. |
| 914 | ◀ | 3772 | Pecan-med. |
| | | Step 2: Backstitch (1 strand) | |
| 42 | | 3350 | Dusty Rose-dk. |

# June Blossoms

**SAMPLE for Basket**

Stitched on driftwood Belfast Linen 32 over 2 threads, the finished design size is 7½" x 8¾". The fabric was cut 14" x 15".

| FABRICS | DESIGN SIZES |
|---|---|
| Aida 11 | 10⅞" x 12¾" |
| Aida 14 | 8⅝" x 10" |
| Aida 18 | 6⅝" x 7¾" |
| Hardanger 22 | 5½" x 6⅜" |

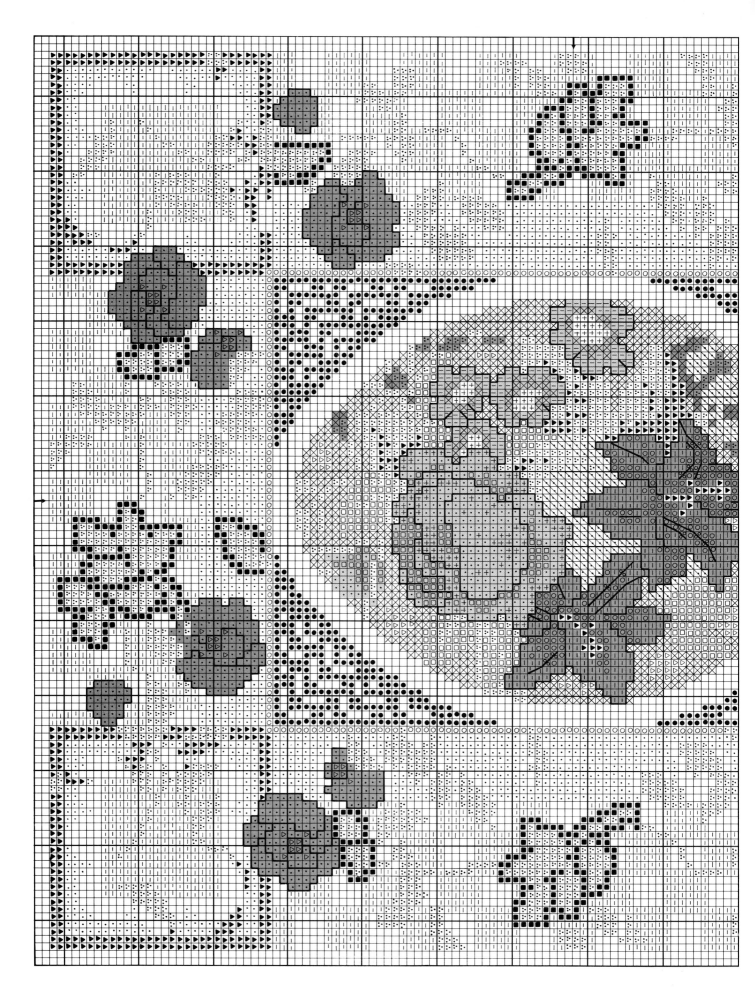

**Stitch Count: 120 x 140**

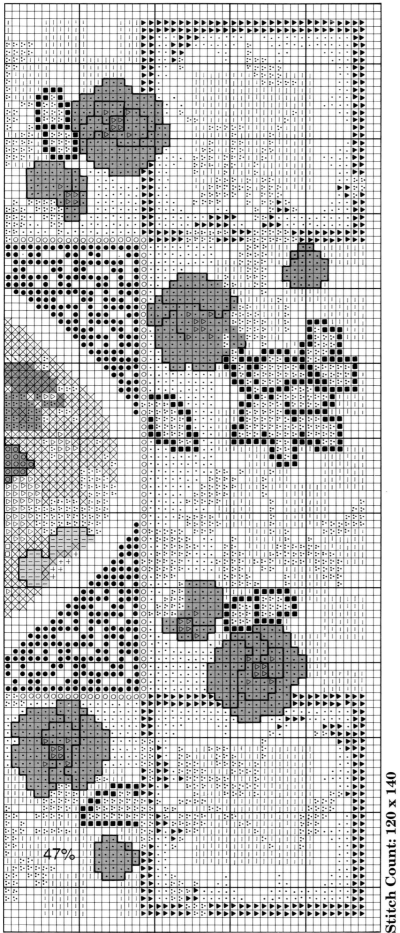

47%

**SAMPLE for Bouquet**
Stitched on driftwood Belfast Linen 32 over 2 threads, the finished design size is 7½" x 8¾". The fabric was cut 14" x 15".

| FABRICS | DESIGN SIZES |
|---|---|
| Aida 11 | 10⅞" x 12¾" |
| Aida 14 | 8⅝" x 10" |
| Aida 18 | 6⅝" x 7¾" |
| Hardanger 22 | 5½" x 6⅞" |

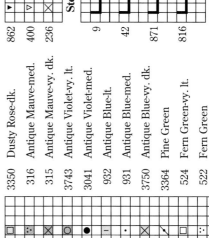

| Anchor | DMC | | |
|---|---|---|---|
| | | | ▶ | 862 | 520 | Fern Green-dk. |
| | | | ▽ | 400 | 317 | Pewter Gray |
| | | | ☒ | 236 | 3799 | Pewter Gray-vy. dk. |

**Step 2: Backstitch (1 strand)**

| Anchor | DMC | |
|---|---|---|
| 9 | 760 | Salmon (salmon flowers) |
| 42 | 3350 | Dusty Rose-dk. (rose) |
| 871 | 3041 | Antique Violet-med. (iris) |
| 816 | 3750 | Antique Blue-vy. dk. (blue flowers) |

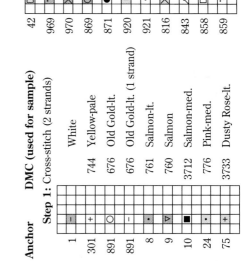

| Anchor | | DMC (used for sample) | |
|---|---|---|---|
| | | **Step 1:** Cross-stitch (2 strands) | |
| 1 | ⊟ | | White |
| 301 | + | 744 | Yellow-pale |
| 891 | ○ | 676 | Old Gold-lt. |
| 891 | − | 676 | Old Gold-lt. (1 strand) |
| 8 | • | 761 | Salmon-lt. |
| 9 | ▽ | 760 | Salmon |
| 10 | ■ | 3712 | Salmon-med. |
| 24 | • | 776 | Pink-med. |
| 75 | + | 3733 | Dusty Rose-lt. |
| 42 | ⊟ | 3350 | Dusty Rose-dk. |
| 969 | ⫶ | 316 | Antique Mauve-med. |
| 970 | ☒ | 315 | Antique Mauve-vy. dk. |
| 869 | ○ | 3743 | Antique Violet-vy. lt. |
| 871 | ● | 3041 | Antique Violet-med. |
| 920 | − | 932 | Antique Blue-lt. |
| 921 | • | 931 | Antique Blue-med. |
| 816 | ☒ | 3750 | Antique Blue-vy. dk. |
| 843 | ╱ | 3364 | Pine Green |
| 858 | ☐ | 524 | Fern Green-vy. lt. |
| 859 | ⫶ | 522 | Fern Green |

## JUNE 12

# Children's Day

*Massachusetts sets aside the second Sunday of June to honor its youngest citizens. This little one, stitched in soft pastels with a touch of glitter, wishes on a star and symbolizes our bright hopes for all children.*

## Wish on a Star

### SAMPLE

Stitched on light blue Jobelan 28 over 2 threads, the finished design size is 4½" x 6¾". The fabric was cut 11" x 13". See page 142 for Balger blending filament.

| FABRICS | DESIGN SIZES |
|---|---|
| Aida 11 | 5¾" x 8⅝" |
| Aida 14 | 4½" x 6¾" |
| Aida 18 | 3½" x 5¼" |
| Hardanger 22 | 2⅞" x 4⅜" |

**Stitch Count: 63 x 95**

| Anchor | | | DMC | (used for sample) |
|---|---|---|---|---|

**Step 1: Cross-stitch (2 strands)**

| 300 | – | ╱ | 745 | Yellow-lt. pale |
| 306 | ○ | ◔ | 725 | Topaz |
| 4146 | + | ╱ | 754 | Peach-lt. |
| 8 | ∴ | | 353 | Peach |
| 49 | • | | 963 | Wild Rose-vy. lt. |
| 50 | ○ | ◔ | 3716 | Wild Rose-lt. |
| 76 | ✕ | ╳ | 962 | Wild Rose-med. |
| 158 | + | ╱ | 3756 | Baby Blue-ultra vy. lt. |

| 121 | ▫ | ◩ | 793 | Cornflower Blue-med. |
| 121 | | | 793 | Cornflower Blue-med. (1 strand) |
| | ∴ | | 014 | Sky Blue Balger blending filament (2 strands) |
| 204 | • | ╱ | 912 | Emerald Green-lt. |
| 210 | ✕ | ╱ | 562 | Jade-med. |
| 189 | ■ | ◤ | 991 | Aquamarine-dk. |
| 347 | ▨ | ╱ | 402 | Mahogany-vy. lt. |
| 338 | ✕ | ╱ | 3776 | Mahogany-lt. |
| 379 | ▣ | ◩ | 840 | Beige Brown-med. |
| 380 | ∴ | ╱ | 839 | Beige Brown-dk. |

**Step 2: Backstitch (1 strand)**

| 121 | | 793 | Cornflower Blue-med. |
| | | 014 | Sky Blue Balger blending filament (sky, 2 strands) |
| 379 | | 840 | Beige Brown-med. (moon) |
| 380 | | 839 | Beige Brown-dk. (all else) |

**Step 3: French Knot (1 strand)**

| 379 | ● | 840 | Beige Brown-med. (moon) |
| 380 | ▲ | 839 | Beige Brown-dk. (girl) |

**67**

JUNE 19

# *Father's Day*

*Whether sitting behind a desk, playing catch, or bandaging a skinned knee, Dad's a real hero. Take time to honor the world's best father on his special day with this handsome Western-motif desk set.*

# For Our Hero

## SAMPLE
## for Diamond Border

Stitched on amber Linen 28 over 2 threads, the finished design size for 1 repeat is 2⅝" x 1⅛". See Steps 1–3 of Directions before purchasing, cutting, and stitching fabric.

| FABRICS | DESIGN SIZES |
|---|---|
| Aida 11 | 3¼" x 1⅜" |
| Aida 14 | 2⅝" x 1⅛" |
| Aida 18 | 2" x ⅞" |
| Hardanger 22 | 1⅝" x ⅝" |

## SAMPLE
## for Buffalo Border

Stitched on amber Linen 28 over 2 threads, the finished design size for 1 repeat is 5¼" x 2¾". See Steps 1–3 of Directions before purchasing, cutting, and stitching fabric.

| FABRICS | DESIGN SIZES |
|---|---|
| Aida 11 | 6⅝" x 3½" |
| Aida 14 | 5¼" x 2¾" |
| Aida 18 | 4" x 2⅛" |
| Hardanger 22 | 3⅜" x 1¾" |

## SAMPLE
## for Moose Border

Stitched on amber Linen 28 over 2 threads, the finished design size for 1 repeat is 4" x 2⅛". See Steps 1–3 of Directions before purchasing, cutting, and stitching fabric.

| FABRICS | DESIGN SIZES |
|---|---|
| Aida 11 | 5⅛" x 2⅝" |
| Aida 14 | 4" x 2⅛" |
| Aida 18 | 3⅛" x 1⅝" |
| Hardanger 22 | 2½" x 1⅜" |

## MATERIALS

Completed cross-stitch designs on amber Linen 28; matching thread
Purchased desk set

## DIRECTIONS

All seam allowances are ¼".

**1.** For 1 desk piece, before stitching, measure perimeter of desk piece. Add 6" to horizontal and vertical measurements. Cut unstitched fabric to match measurements.

**2.** Center chosen design vertically and begin stitching first motif 1" from 1 end of fabric. Repeat motif across fabric, leaving 1" unstitched at opposite end.

**3.** For Diamond Border, trim long edges of fabric to 1" above and below design. For Buffalo Border, trim long edges of fabric to 2" above and below design. For Moose Border, trim long edges of fabric to 1¾" above and below design.

**4.** With right sides facing and raw edges aligned, fold design piece in half. Stitch long raw edges together to make a tube. Turn. Position seam in center back and press.

**5.** Fold ends of design piece under ¼" and press. Wrap band snugly around desk set piece, overlapping ends and aligning long edges and motifs. Slip-stitch ends together. Repeat for remaining desk pieces.

## Stitches to Go On

These Western images will also suit your littlest buckaroo. Use waste canvas to add a moose border to his pillowcases or a few buffalo to bath towels. Or stitch the motifs on some Western overalls.

| Anchor | | DMC (used for sample) | |
|---|---|---|---|
| | Step 1: Cross-stitch (2 strands) | | |
| 921 | | 931 | Antique Blue-med. |
| 779 | | 926 | Slate Green |
| 246 | | 319 | Pistachio Green-vy. dk. |
| 879 | | 500 | Blue Green-vy. dk. |
| 351 | | 400 | Mahogany-dk. |
| 352 | | 300 | Mahogany-vy. dk. |
| 381 | | 838 | Beige Brown-vy. dk. |
| | Step 2: Backstitch (1 strand) | | |
| 381 | | 838 | Beige Brown-vy. dk. |

## Diamond Border

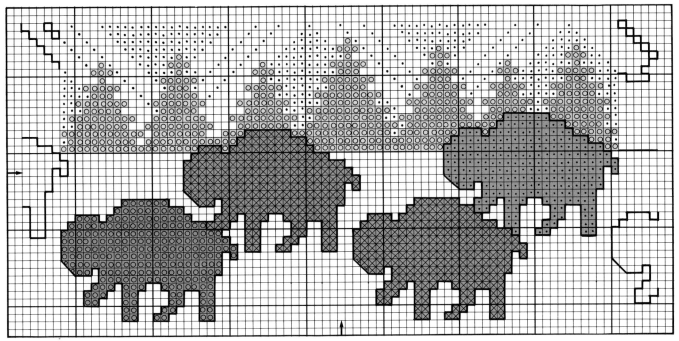

**Stitch Count: 36 x 15 (for 1 repeat)**

## Buffalo Border

**Stitch Count: 73 x 39 (for 1 repeat)**

## Moose Border

**Stitch Count: 56 x 29 (for 1 repeat)**

# First Day
# of Summer

*In northern climes, the bears are the first*
*to know when the huckleberries ripen.*
*It's summertime!*
*There's nothing lazy or hazy about*
*these busy days of berry gathering*
*in the warm sunshine.*

# Huckleberries

**SAMPLE**
Stitched on white Aida 14 over 1 thread, the finished design size is 9" x 7⅜". The fabric was cut 15" x 14". See page 140 for framing ideas.

| FABRICS | DESIGN SIZES |
|---|---|
| Aida 11 | 11½" x 9½" |
| Aida 18 | 7" x 5¾" |
| Hardanger 22 | 5¾" x 4¾" |

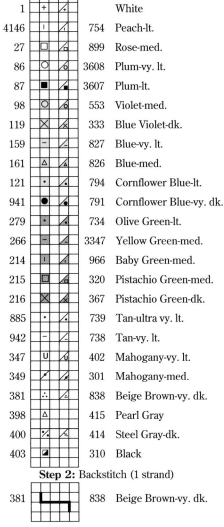

| Anchor | | | DMC | (used for sample) |
|---|---|---|---|---|
| **Step 1:** Cross-stitch (2 strands) | | | | |
| 1 | + | | | White |
| 4146 | | | 754 | Peach-lt. |
| 27 | | | 899 | Rose-med. |
| 86 | O | | 3608 | Plum-vy. lt. |
| 87 | ■ | | 3607 | Plum-lt. |
| 98 | O | | 553 | Violet-med. |
| 119 | X | | 333 | Blue Violet-dk. |
| 159 | – | | 827 | Blue-vy. lt. |
| 161 | ▲ | | 826 | Blue-med. |
| 121 | · | | 794 | Cornflower Blue-lt. |
| 941 | ● | | 791 | Cornflower Blue-vy. dk. |
| 279 | | | 734 | Olive Green-lt. |
| 266 | – | | 3347 | Yellow Green-med. |
| 214 | | | 966 | Baby Green-med. |
| 215 | | | 320 | Pistachio Green-med. |
| 216 | X | | 367 | Pistachio Green-dk. |
| 885 | · | | 739 | Tan-ultra vy. lt. |
| 942 | – | | 738 | Tan-vy. lt. |
| 347 | U | | 402 | Mahogany-vy. lt. |
| 349 | ⁄ | | 301 | Mahogany-med. |
| 381 | ∴ | | 838 | Beige Brown-vy. dk. |
| 398 | ▲ | | 415 | Pearl Gray |
| 400 | ⁒ | | 414 | Steel Gray-dk. |
| 403 | ◪ | | 310 | Black |
| **Step 2:** Backstitch (1 strand) | | | | |
| 381 | | | 838 | Beige Brown-vy. dk. |

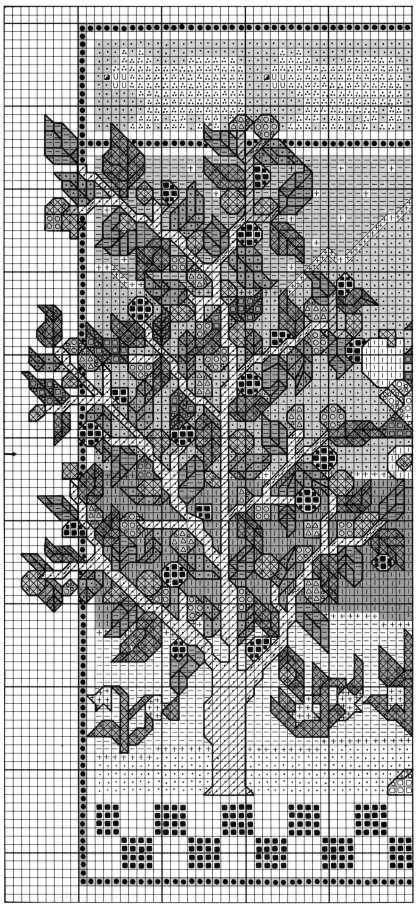

**Stitch Count: 126 x 104**

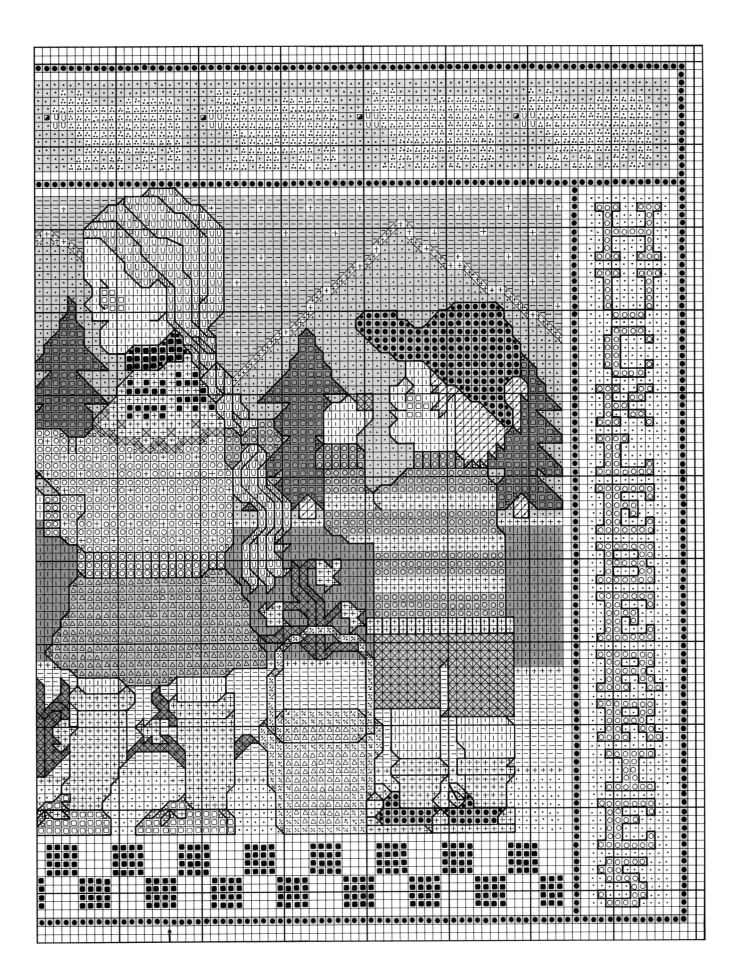

# Spirit of America Day

*The citizens of Decatur, Alabama, began this red-white-and-blue celebration in 1966, and it's still going strong. Salute the sentiment with a sampler starring all things American at heart.*

**Stitch Count: 108 x 146**

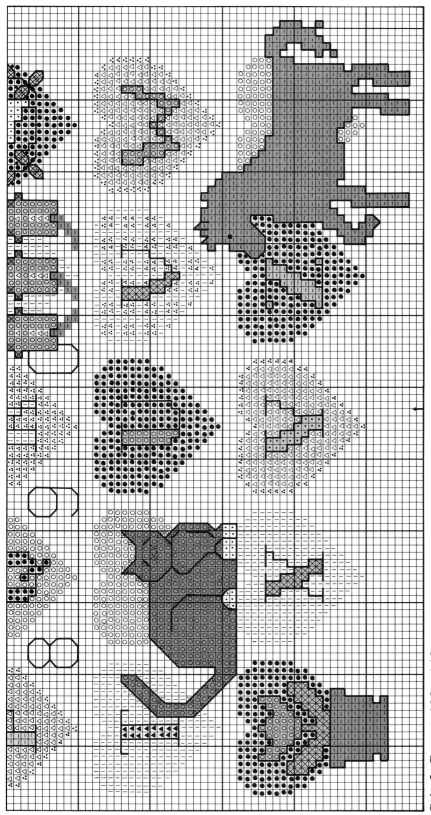

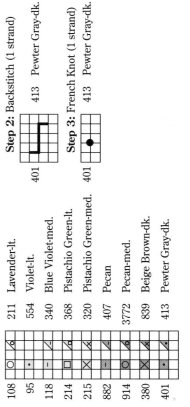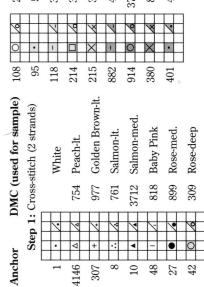

| Anchor | DMC (used for sample) | | |
|---|---|---|---|
| | Step 1: Cross-stitch (2 strands) | | |
| 1 | | | White |
| 4146 | | 754 | Peach-lt. |
| 307 | | 977 | Golden Brown-lt. |
| 8 | | 761 | Salmon-lt. |
| 10 | | 3712 | Salmon-med. |
| 48 | | 818 | Baby Pink |
| 27 | | 899 | Rose-med. |
| 42 | | 309 | Rose-deep |
| 108 | | 211 | Lavender-lt. |
| 95 | | 554 | Violet-lt. |
| 118 | | 340 | Blue Violet-med. |
| 214 | | 368 | Pistachio Green-lt. |
| 215 | | 320 | Pistachio Green-med. |
| 882 | | 407 | Pecan |
| 914 | | 3772 | Pecan-med. |
| 380 | | 839 | Beige Brown-dk. |
| 401 | | 413 | Pewter Gray-dk. |

**Step 2: Backstitch (1 strand)**

401  413  Pewter Gray-dk.

**Step 3: French Knot (1 strand)**

401  413  Pewter Gray-dk.

# Heart of America

**SAMPLE**
Stitched on white Aida 14 over 1 thread, the finished design size is 7¾" x 10⅜". The fabric was cut 14" x 17".

**FABRICS**  **DESIGN SIZES**
Aida 11  9⅞" x 13¼"
Aida 18  6" x 8⅛"
Hardanger 22  4⅞" x 6⅝"

# Independence Day

*Remember the glorious Fourth and America's colonial origins with this primitive cross-stitched flag. Its aged look is easily achieved by alternating strips of linen and the reverse of a blue plaid fabric. Create a patriotic frame with weathered lumber you've spangled with stars.*

## Folk Art Flag

### SAMPLE for Heart

Stitched on amber Linen 28 over 2 threads, the finished design size is 5¾" x 5¾". The fabric was cut 12" x 12". (Some motifs in heart design will be used to stitch flag stripes. See Steps 1 and 2 of Directions before cutting and stitching.) See page 140 for framing ideas.

| FABRICS | DESIGN SIZES |
| --- | --- |
| Aida 11 | 7⅜" x 7⅜" |
| Aida 14 | 5¾" x 5¾" |
| Aida 18 | 4½" x 4½" |
| Hardanger 22 | 3⅝" x 3⅝" |

### MATERIALS

Completed cross-stitch on amber Linen 28; matching thread

½ yard of unstitched amber Linen 28

½ yard of country blue plaid fabric

### DIRECTIONS

All seam allowances are ¼".

**1.** For heart, with design centered, trim design piece to 7¾" square.

**2.** From unstitched linen, cut 2 (6" x 20") strips and 3 (6" x 26") strips. On 1 (6" x 20") strip and 2 (6" x 26") strips, center and stitch house-and-tree motif to fill, leaving approximately 3" of unstitched fabric at each end. On remaining 6" x 20" strip, center and stitch goose motif to fill. On remaining 6" x 26" strip, center and stitch sheep motif to fill.

Stitch checkerboard border 2 threads above and below each design. With designs centered, trim width of each strip to 3".

**3.** From plaid fabric, cut 2 (1¾" x 20") strips and 2 (1¾" x 26") strips.

**4.** Referring to photo, with right side of design strips facing wrong side of plaid strips and raw edges aligned, join 20"-long strips by alternating design strips and plaid strips. Trim left edge of joined strips to ½" outside stitched designs.

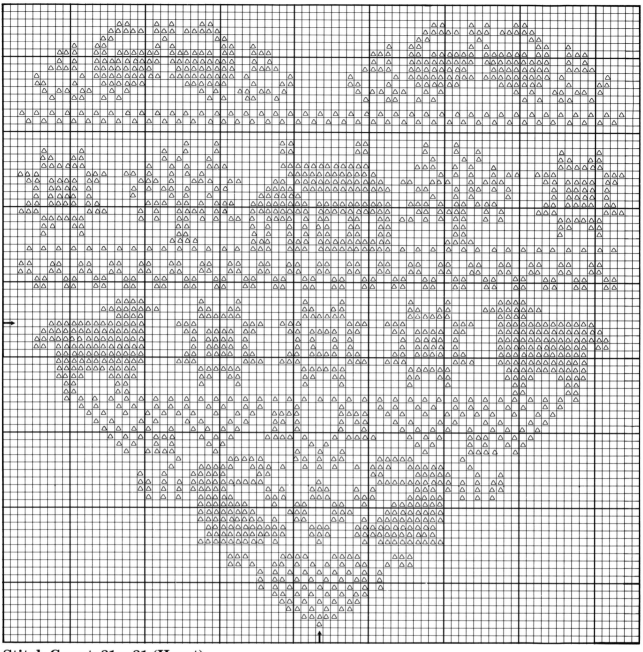

**Stitch Count: 81 x 81 (Heart)**

**5.** With right sides facing and bottom edges aligned, stitch right edge of heart design piece to left edge of joined strips. Set aside.

**6.** Repeat Step 4 to join 26"-long design strips and plaid strips. (*Do not* trim left edge of 26"-long joined strips.)

**7.** With right sides facing and raw edges aligned, stitch top edge of joined 26"-long strips to bottom edge of joined

20"-long strips and heart piece. Using 1 strand of red floss, feather-stitch (see Diagram, page 139) along right and bottom edges of heart square.

Anchor          DMC (used for sample)

**Step 1:** Cross-stitch (2 strands)

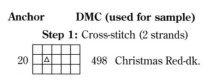

20          498   Christmas Red-dk.

**82**

## AUGUST 20

# *Watermelon Day*

*Although Vining, Minnesota, has a
population of only 87, more than a thousand friends
and visitors gather there each August to enjoy cool,
sweet slices of watermelon. Our red-and-gold
sampler combines cross-stitch with specialty
stitches to celebrate this summer favorite.*

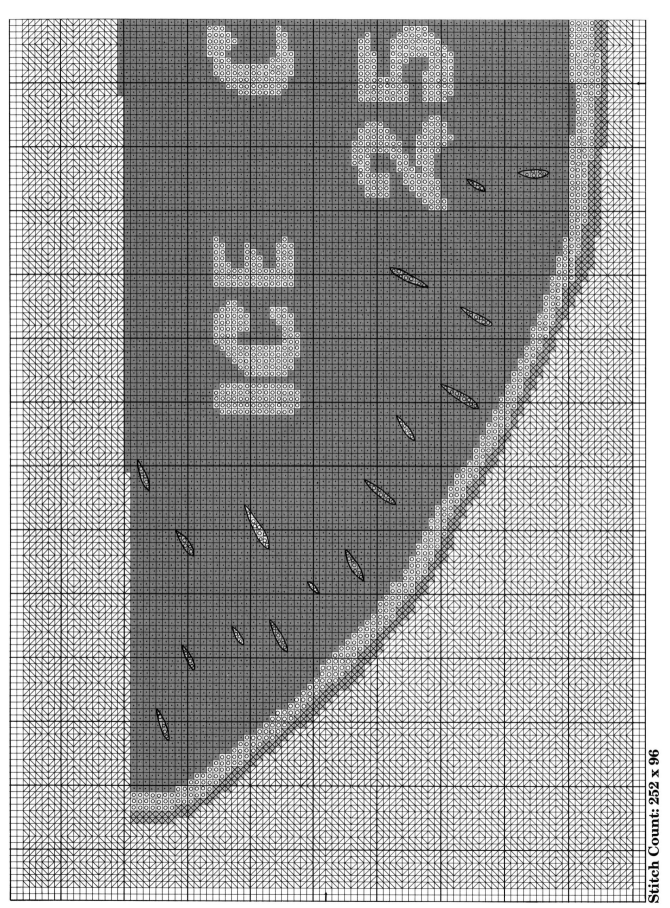

# A Slice of Summer

**SAMPLE**
Stitched on Needlepoint Canvas 14, the finished design size is 18" x 6⅝". The fabric was cut 24" x 13". See page 139 for specialty stitches.

**FABRICS**    **DESIGN SIZES**
Aida 11    23" x 8¾"
Aida 14    18" x 6⅝"
Aida 18    14" x 5⅜"
Hardanger 22    11½" x 4⅜"

**Anchor**    **DMC Pearl Cotton #5**
(used for sample)

**Step 1:** Cross-stitch (2 strands)

| Anchor | DMC | |
|---|---|---|
| 1 | | White |
| 47 | 321 | Christmas Red |
| 246 | 986 | Forest Green-vy. dk. |
| 403 | 310 | Black |

**Step 2:** Scotch Stitch (1 strand)

| 306 | 725 | Topaz |

**Step 3:** Lazy Daisy Stitch (1 strand)

| 1 | | White |
| 403 | 310 | Black |

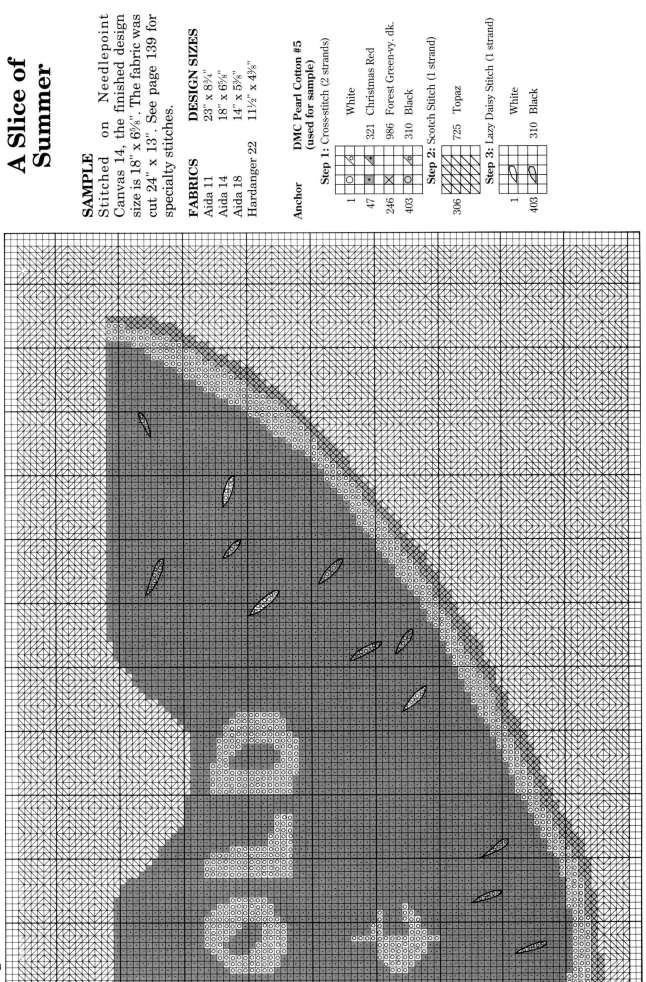

# SEPTEMBER 19

## Harvest Moon

*The bright beams
of the harvest moon
illuminate the fields,
allowing this farmer's wife
extra time to reap the last
bounties of summer.
The mellow colors in
this stitched piece make it
an attractive accent
for the kitchen or
breakfast room.*

## Harvest Basket

**SAMPLE**
Stitched on cream Aida 14 over
1 thread, the finished design
size is 5" x 7". The fabric was
cut 11" x 13".

| FABRICS | DESIGN SIZES |
|---|---|
| Aida 11 | 6⅜" x 8⅞" |
| Aida 18 | 3⅞" x 5½" |
| Hardanger 22 | 3⅛" x 4½" |

**Stitch Count: 70 x 98**

| Anchor | | | DMC (used for sample) | |
|---|---|---|---|---|
| | | | **Step 1:** Cross-stitch (2 strands) | |
| 891 | + | ⊿ | 676 | Old Gold-lt. |
| 880 | ∴ | ⊿ | 948 | Peach-vy. lt. |
| 868 | · | ⊿ | 3779 | Terra Cotta-vy. lt. |
| 337 | △ | | 3778 | Terra Cotta |
| 347 | ▨ | ⊿ | 402 | Mahogany-vy. lt. |
| 338 | ○ | ⊘ | 3776 | Mahogany-lt. |
| 74 | □ | ⊿ | 3354 | Dusty Rose-vy. lt. |
| 76 | ∴ | ⊿ | 3731 | Dusty Rose-med. |

| | | | | |
|---|---|---|---|---|
| 101 | ▲ | ⊿ | 327 | Antique Violet-vy. dk. |
| 158 | I | ⊿ | 775 | Baby Blue-vy. lt. |
| 167 | □ | | 519 | Sky Blue |
| 168 | ⊠ | ⊠ | 518 | Wedgwood-lt. |
| 213 | ○ | ⊘ | 369 | Pistachio Green-vy. lt. |
| 214 | ⊠ | ⊠ | 368 | Pistachio Green-lt. |
| 216 | ● | ⊿ | 367 | Pistachio Green-dk. |
| 363 | · | | 436 | Tan |
| 309 | △ | △ | 435 | Brown-vy. lt. |
| 371 | ⊠ | | 433 | Brown-med. |

| | | | | |
|---|---|---|---|---|
| 379 | – | ⊿ | 840 | Beige Brown-med. |
| 380 | ■ | ⊿ | 839 | Beige Brown-dk. |
| 399 | □ | ⊿ | 318 | Steel Gray-lt. |

**Step 2:** Backstitch (1 strand)

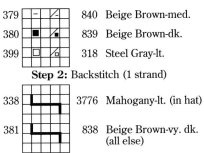

| | | | |
|---|---|---|---|
| 338 | | 3776 | Mahogany-lt. (in hat) |
| 381 | | 838 | Beige Brown-vy. dk. (all else) |

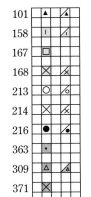

---

❋

# *First Day of*
# *Autumn*

*Drifting leaves and cozy sweaters signal the
golden season of autumn. Ripening pumpkins will
no doubt become shining jack-o'-lanterns
that welcome friends inside.*

---

# Pumpkins

## SAMPLE

Stitched on Rustico 14 over 1 thread, the finished design size is 9⅛" x 7⅜". The fabric was cut 16" x 14".

| FABRICS | DESIGN SIZES |
|---|---|
| Aida 11 | 11⅝" x 9⅜" |
| Aida 14 | 9⅛" x 7⅜" |
| Aida 18 | 7⅛" x 5¾" |
| Hardanger 22 | 5⅞" x 4⅝" |

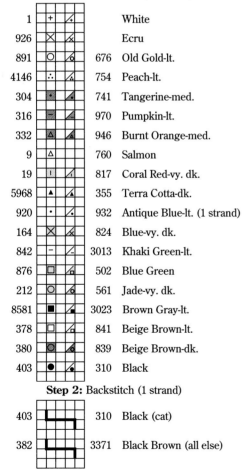

| Anchor | | | DMC | (used for sample) |
|---|---|---|---|---|
| **Step 1:** | **Cross-stitch (2 strands)** | | | |
| 1 | + | | | White |
| 926 | X | | | Ecru |
| 891 | O | | 676 | Old Gold-lt. |
| 4146 | | | 754 | Peach-lt. |
| 304 | | | 741 | Tangerine-med. |
| 316 | | | 970 | Pumpkin-lt. |
| 332 | △ | | 946 | Burnt Orange-med. |
| 9 | △ | | 760 | Salmon |
| 19 | I | | 817 | Coral Red-vy. dk. |
| 5968 | ▲ | | 355 | Terra Cotta-dk. |
| 920 | · | | 932 | Antique Blue-lt. (1 strand) |
| 164 | X | | 824 | Blue-vy. dk. |
| 842 | − | | 3013 | Khaki Green-lt. |
| 876 | □ | | 502 | Blue Green |
| 212 | O | | 561 | Jade-vy. dk. |
| 8581 | ■ | | 3023 | Brown Gray-lt. |
| 378 | □ | | 841 | Beige Brown-lt. |
| 380 | ● | | 839 | Beige Brown-dk. |
| 403 | ● | | 310 | Black |
| **Step 2:** | **Backstitch (1 strand)** | | | |
| 403 | | | 310 | Black (cat) |
| 382 | | | 3371 | Black Brown (all else) |

**Stitch Count: 128 x 103**

91

## OCTOBER

# *National Clock Month*

*As October arrives, daylight hours grow shorter. Mark the passing of the days by stitching our fruited still life for this timeless clock, a combination of precision technology and your creativity.*

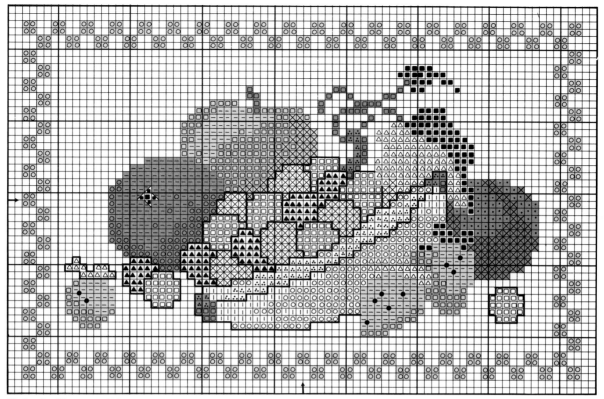

**Stitch Count: 78 x 50**

# A Stitch in Time

## SAMPLE

Stitched on cream Hardanger 22 over 2 threads, the finished design size is 7⅛" x 4½". The fabric was cut 12" x 10". See page 142 for clock. (*Note:* Instructions and measurements are for clock used in sample. If using another clock, adjust as necessary.)

| FABRICS | DESIGN SIZES |
|---------|--------------|
| Aida 11 | 7⅛" x 4½" |
| Aida 14 | 5⅝" x 3⅝" |
| Aida 18 | 4⅜" x 2¾" |

## MATERIALS

Completed cross-stitch on cream Hardanger 22
2 (12" x 10") pieces of thin polyester batting
1 (8⅛" x 5⅞") piece of heavy-weight mat board
Liquid ravel preventer
Hot-glue gun and glue sticks
Purchased clock

## DIRECTIONS

**1.** Apply liquid ravel preventer to raw edges of design piece; let dry.

**2.** Center batting pieces on mat board. Fold batting to back of board and glue both layers to secure.

**3.** Center design piece horizontally on batting layers, with bottom of design 1¼" from bottom edge of mat board. Keeping tension even on all sides, fold design piece to back and glue to secure.

**4.** Insert design piece into bottom of clock (see photo).

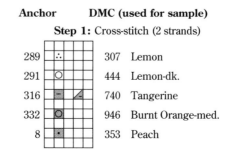

| Anchor | | DMC (used for sample) | |
|--------|--|------------------------|--|

**Step 1:** Cross-stitch (2 strands)

| 289 | | 307 | Lemon |
| 291 | | 444 | Lemon-dk. |
| 316 | | 740 | Tangerine |
| 332 | | 946 | Burnt Orange-med. |
| 8 | | 353 | Peach |

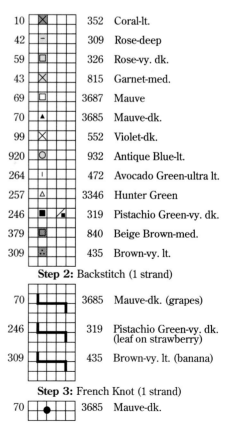

| 10 | | 352 | Coral-lt. |
| 42 | | 309 | Rose-deep |
| 59 | | 326 | Rose-vy. dk. |
| 43 | | 815 | Garnet-med. |
| 69 | | 3687 | Mauve |
| 70 | | 3685 | Mauve-dk. |
| 99 | | 552 | Violet-dk. |
| 920 | | 932 | Antique Blue-lt. |
| 264 | | 472 | Avocado Green-ultra lt. |
| 257 | | 3346 | Hunter Green |
| 246 | | 319 | Pistachio Green-vy. dk. |
| 379 | | 840 | Beige Brown-med. |
| 309 | | 435 | Brown-vy. lt. |

**Step 2:** Backstitch (1 strand)

| 70 | | 3685 | Mauve-dk. (grapes) |
| 246 | | 319 | Pistachio Green-vy. dk. (leaf on strawberry) |
| 309 | | 435 | Brown-vy. lt. (banana) |

**Step 3:** French Knot (1 strand)

| 70 | | 3685 | Mauve-dk. |

OCTOBER 31

# *Halloween*

*Stitch a whimsical witch and
her bubbling brew on this wickedly colorful
banner. Hang it on your front door to
welcome trick-or-treaters of all ages.*

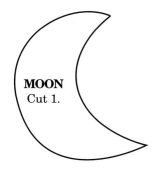

**MOON**
Cut 1.

**STAR**
Cut 1.

## Trick-or-Treat Banner

### SAMPLE
Stitched on amaretto Murano 30 over 2 threads, the finished design size is 4⅝" x 11⅛". The fabric was cut 10" x 19".

| FABRICS | DESIGN SIZES |
|---|---|
| Aida 11 | 6⅜" x 15⅛" |
| Aida 14 | 5" x 11⅞" |
| Aida 18 | 3⅞" x 9¼" |
| Hardanger 22 | 3⅛" x 7½" |

### MATERIALS
Completed cross-stitch on amaretto Murano 30; matching thread
¼ yard of unstitched amaretto Murano 30
¼ yard of thin polyester batting
32½" (¼") black piping
2¼ yards of DMC #3 black Pearl Cotton
1 (6"-long) black tassel

1 (2"-square) piece of ⅜"-thick plywood or ¾"-thick foam-core board
Jigsaw or craft knife
Drill with ¼" bit
Sandpaper
8" (¼"-diameter) dowel
Acrylic paints: yellow, black
Paintbrush
Hot-glue gun and glue sticks
Tracing paper
Liquid ravel preventer
Dressmaker's pen

### DIRECTIONS
All seam allowances are ¼".

**1.** Transfer patterns to tracing paper and cut out. With design centered and bottom point of design 1⅜" above bottom point of pattern, transfer banner pattern to design piece and cut out. From unstitched Murano, cut 1 banner piece for backing. From batting, cut 2 banner pieces.

**2.** Baste 1 batting piece to wrong side of design piece. With right sides facing and raw edges aligned, stitch piping to side and bottom edges of design piece, rounding corners slightly. Trim batting from seam allowance.

**3.** Baste remaining batting piece to wrong side of backing. With right sides facing and raw edges aligned, stitch design piece to backing, sewing along stitching line of piping and leaving top edge open for turning. Trim corners and turn. To make casing, turn top raw edge under ½" and press. Turn folded edge 1¼" to back and slipstitch in place.

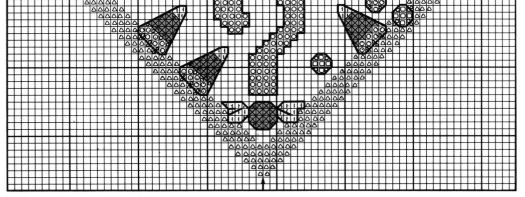

**Stitch Count: 70 x 166**

---

↑ Extend banner 12". ↑

**BANNER**
Cut 1 from design piece and
1 from unstitched Murano.
Cut 2 from batting.
Add ¼" seam allowances.

**4.** Transfer star and moon patterns to plywood. Using jigsaw, cut out. Referring to photo, drill 1 (¼"-deep) hole into 1 side of each cutout. Sand cutouts smooth. (If using foam-core board, transfer patterns to foam core. Using craft knife, cut out. *Do not* drill holes in foam core.) Paint cutouts yellow and dowel black. Let dry.

**5.** Insert dowel through casing. Glue star and moon to each end of dowel. (If using foam-core cutouts, insert dowel ¼" into foam core and glue.)

**6.** To make hanger, cut 4 (20") lengths from pearl cotton. Handling all lengths as 1, knot at each end of dowel. Trim ends and apply liquid ravel preventer to knots. Tack tassel to piping at center bottom of banner.

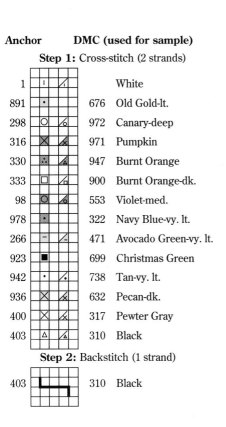

**Stitches to Go On**

This small banner would look terrific hung from the center of a grapevine wreath. Use waste canvas to stitch the design on a trick-or-treat bag for a child or add it to a grown-up's sweatshirt.

| Anchor | | | DMC (used for sample) | |
|---|---|---|---|---|
| **Step 1:** Cross-stitch (2 strands) | | | | |
| 1 | ı | ⁄ | | White |
| 891 | · | ⁄ | 676 | Old Gold-lt. |
| 298 | O | ⁄ | 972 | Canary-deep |
| 316 | ⊠ | ⁄ | 971 | Pumpkin |
| 330 | ∴ | ⁄ | 947 | Burnt Orange |
| 333 | □ | ⁄ | 900 | Burnt Orange-dk. |
| 98 | ⊙ | ⁄ | 553 | Violet-med. |
| 978 | ▪ | ⁄ | 322 | Navy Blue-vy. lt. |
| 266 | − | ⁄ | 471 | Avocado Green-vy. lt. |
| 923 | ■ | ⁄ | 699 | Christmas Green |
| 942 | · | ⁄ | 738 | Tan-vy. lt. |
| 936 | ⊠ | ⁄ | 632 | Pecan-dk. |
| 400 | ⊠ | ⁄ | 317 | Pewter Gray |
| 403 | △ | ⁄ | 310 | Black |
| **Step 2:** Backstitch (1 strand) | | | | |
| 403 | | | 310 | Black |

# The First Thanksgiving

*Native Americans have shared many aspects
of their culture, including the practice of
decorating their homes and clothing with
intricate geometrics. These handsome pillows
recall some of those unique designs.*

## A Proud Heritage

**SAMPLE for Small Pillow**
Stitched on dirty linen Dublin Linen 25 over 2 threads, the finished design size is 8½" x 8½". The fabric was cut 14" x 14".

| FABRICS | DESIGN SIZES |
| --- | --- |
| Aida 11 | 9¾" x 9¾" |
| Aida 14 | 7⅝" x 7⅝" |
| Aida 18 | 6" x 6" |
| Hardanger 22 | 4⅞" x 4⅞" |

**MATERIALS (for 1 small pillow)**
Completed cross-stitch on dirty linen Dublin Linen 25
¾ yard of burgundy fabric; matching thread
⅛ yard of contrasting print fabric; matching thread
⅜ yard of polyester fleece
6⅞ yards (¼") cording
Stuffing
Bodkin

**DIRECTIONS**
All seam allowances are ¼".

**1.** With design centered, trim design piece to 11" square.

**2.** From burgundy fabric, cut 1 (11") square for pillow back and 3 (3" x 45") strips for shirring. From remainder, cut 1½"-wide strips, piecing as needed to equal 5 yards. From print fabric, cut 1½"-wide strips, piecing as needed to equal 66". From fleece, cut 2 (11") squares.

**3.** Baste 1 fleece square to wrong side of design piece and remaining fleece square to wrong side of pillow back.

**4.** For shirring, stitch short raw edges of 3" x 45" strips together to make 1 large circle. Fold circle into fourths widthwise and mark to match pillow corners. Run gathering threads along each long edge and pull to gather threads tightly.

**5.** With right sides facing and raw edges aligned, pin 1 gathered edge of shirring to design piece, adjusting fullness as necessary to match marks to corners. Stitch. With right sides facing and raw edges aligned, stitch remaining gathered edge of shirring to back, leaving an opening for turning. Turn and stuff pillow firmly. Slipstitch opening closed.

**6.** To make corded tubing, cut 1 (5-yard) length and 1 (66") length from cording. With right sides facing and raw edges aligned, fold pieced burgundy strip in half lengthwise. Stitch long raw edges together to make a tube. Turn. Using bodkin, draw 5-yard length of cording through tube. Repeat with pieced print strip and 66" length of cording to make 66" of corded print tubing.

**7.** From burgundy tubing, cut 1 (66") length. Twist 66" lengths of burgundy and print tubing together and tack at each end to secure. Tack twisted tubing along top edge of pillow, covering seam.

**8.** For corners of pillow, cut 4 (30") lengths from remaining burgundy tubing. To make 1 chain, double 1 piece of tubing and knot ends together. Refer to Diagrams to complete chain. Turning ends of chain under, tack 1 end to front at 1 corner of design piece (see photo) and other end to back. Repeat with remaining lengths of tubing.

## SAMPLE for Large Pillow
Stitched on dirty linen Dublin Linen 25 over 2 threads, the finished design size is 14⅝" x 14⅝". The fabric was cut 20" x 20".

| FABRICS | DESIGN SIZES |
|---|---|
| Aida 11 | 16⅝" x 16⅝" |
| Aida 14 | 13⅛" x 13⅛" |
| Aida 18 | 10⅛" x 10⅛" |
| Hardanger 22 | 8⅜" x 8⅜" |

## MATERIALS (for 1 large pillow)
Completed cross-stitch on dirty linen Dublin Linen 25
1¼ yards of blue print fabric; matching thread
⅜ yard of burgundy fabric; matching thread
½ yard of polyester fleece
16 yards (¼") cording, cut in half
Stuffing
Bodkin

## DIRECTIONS
All seam allowances are ¼".

**1.** With design centered, trim design piece to 17" square.

**2.** From blue print fabric, cut 1 (17") square for pillow back and 5 (4½" x 45") strips for shirring. From remainder, cut 1½"-wide strips, piecing as needed to equal 8 yards. From burgundy fabric, cut 1½"-wide strips, piecing as needed to equal 8 yards. Cut 2 (17") squares of fleece.

**3.** Repeat Steps 3–5 of Small Pillow, using 4½" x 45" strips for shirring.

**4.** For corded tubing, refer to Step 6 of Small Pillow to make 8 yards each of burgundy and print tubing.

**5.** For twisted tubing, cut 1 (102") length each of burgundy and print tubing and complete Step 7 of Small Pillow.

**6.** From remaining tubing, cut 4 (45") lengths from each color. To make 1 chain, knot together ends of 1 burgundy length and 1 print length. Refer to Diagrams to complete chain. Turning ends of chain under, tack 1 end to front at 1 corner of design piece (see photo) and other end to back. Repeat with remaining lengths of tubing.

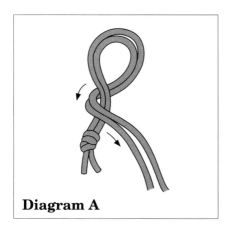

**Diagram A**

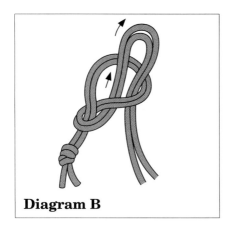

**Diagram B**

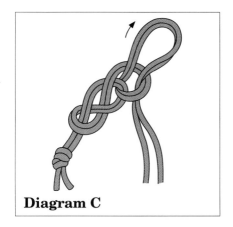

**Diagram C**

**Stitch Count: 107 x 107 (Small Pillow)**

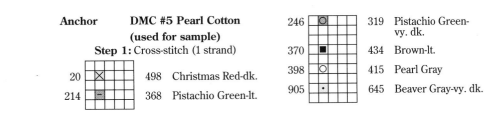

| Anchor | | DMC #5 Pearl Cotton (used for sample) | |
|---|---|---|---|
| **Step 1:** Cross-stitch (1 strand) | | | |
| 20 | ✗ | 498 | Christmas Red-dk. |
| 214 | ▨ | 368 | Pistachio Green-lt. |
| 246 | ◉ | 319 | Pistachio Green-vy. dk. |
| 370 | ■ | 434 | Brown-lt. |
| 398 | ○ | 415 | Pearl Gray |
| 905 | · | 645 | Beaver Gray-vy. dk. |

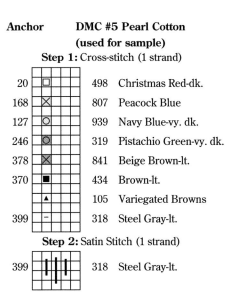

**Anchor**     **DMC #5 Pearl Cotton**
              **(used for sample)**

**Step 1:** Cross-stitch (1 strand)

| 20  | □ | 498 | Christmas Red-dk. |
| 168 | ⊠ | 807 | Peacock Blue |
| 127 | ○ | 939 | Navy Blue-vy. dk. |
| 246 | ◉ | 319 | Pistachio Green-vy. dk. |
| 378 | ⊠ | 841 | Beige Brown-lt. |
| 370 | ■ | 434 | Brown-lt. |
|     | ▲ | 105 | Variegated Browns |
| 399 | – | 318 | Steel Gray-lt. |

**Step 2:** Satin Stitch (1 strand)

| 399 | ‖ | 318 | Steel Gray-lt. |

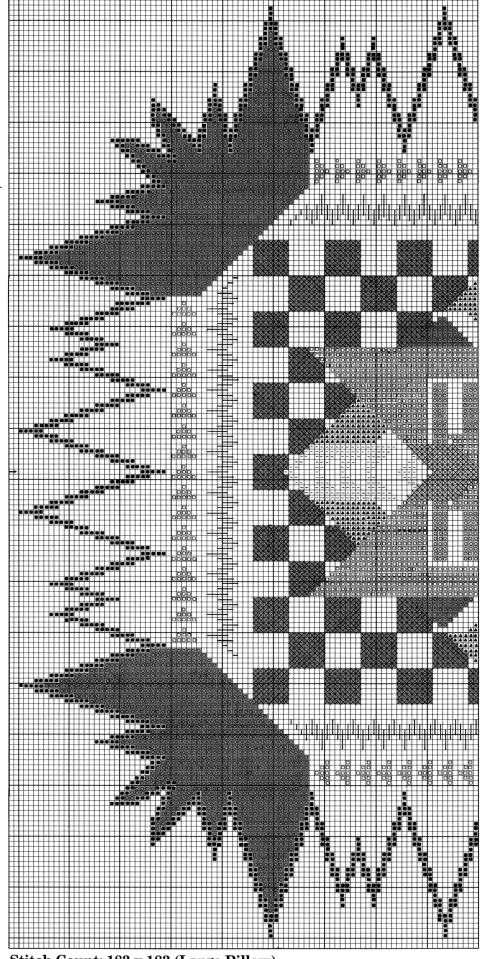

**102**

**Stitch Count: 183 x 183 (Large Pillow)**

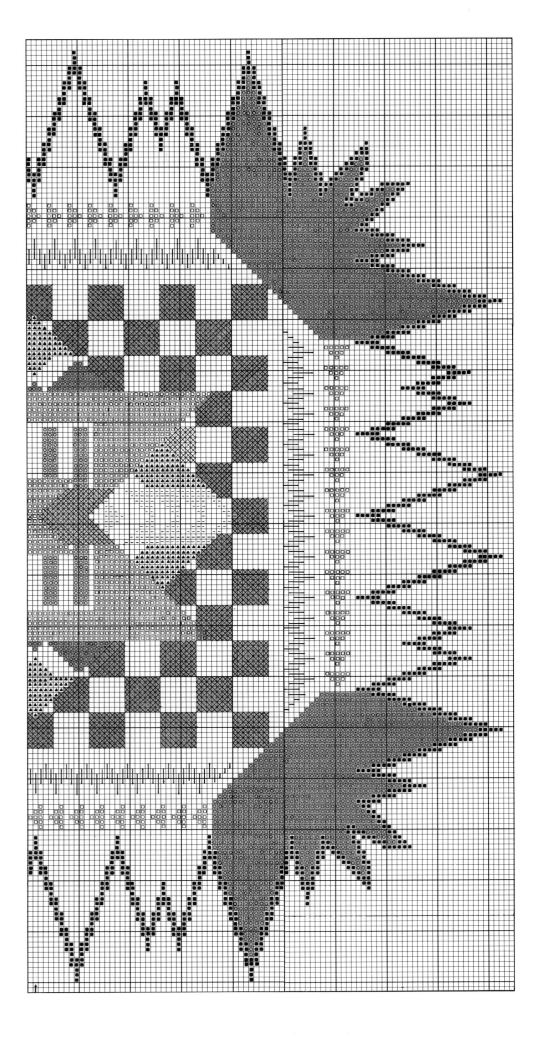

103

# Thanksgiving

*Set your Thanksgiving table with linens you've stitched with classic harvest colors and motifs. Complete the look with matching napkins you can quickly stencil to imitate cross-stitch.*

# Tabletop Bounty

## SAMPLE for Place Mat

Stitched on Vanessa-Ann Afghan Weave 18 over 2 threads, the finished design sizes are 2⅛" x 4⅞" for Pumpkins and 1⅝" x 1⅝" for Leaf. The fabric was cut 22" x 15" (finished width measurement includes 2 whole blocks and ½ block on each side; finished height measurement includes 1 whole block and ½ block at top and bottom). Stitching area of each woven block is 88 x 88 threads. See Diagram for placement. See page 142 for afghan material.

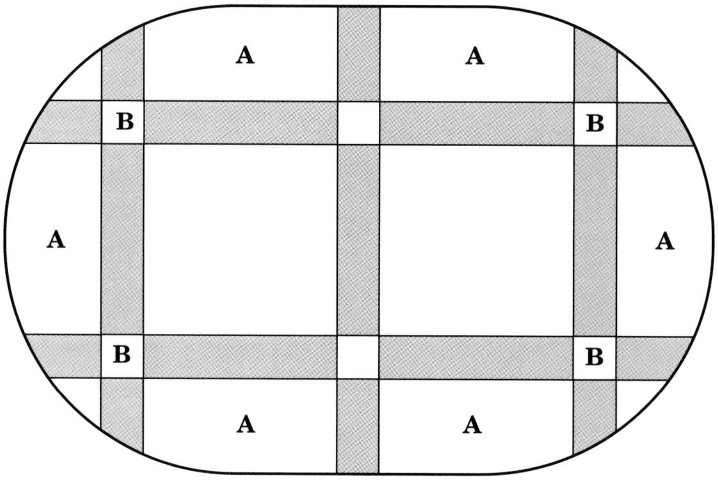

**Placement Diagram**

### Pumpkins

| FABRICS | DESIGN SIZES |
|---|---|
| Aida 11 | 1¾" x 4" |
| Aida 14 | 1⅜" x 3⅛" |
| Aida 18 | 1" x 2½" |
| Hardanger 22 | ⅞" x 2" |

### Leaf

| FABRICS | DESIGN SIZES |
|---|---|
| Aida 11 | 1¼" x 1¼" |
| Aida 14 | 1" x 1" |
| Aida 18 | ¾" x ¾" |
| Hardanger 22 | ⅝" x ⅝" |

## MATERIALS (for 1 place mat)

Completed cross-stitch on Vanessa-Ann Afghan Weave 18; matching thread
½ yard of mustard yellow fabric; matching thread
1 (18½" x 11½") piece of fusible knit interfacing
1½ yards (⅛") cording
Tracing paper

## DIRECTIONS

All seam allowances are ¼".

**1.** Fold tracing paper into fourths. Transfer pattern (page 109) to tracing paper, adding ¼" seam allowance, and cut out. Unfold and set aside.

**2.** With design centered, trim completed design piece to 18½" x 11½". Following the manufacturer's instructions, fuse interfacing to wrong side of design piece. With design centered, transfer pattern to design piece and cut 1. From mustard yellow fabric, cut 1 piece for backing.

**3.** From remaining mustard yellow fabric, cut 1¼"-wide bias strips, piecing as needed to equal 1½ yards. Using pieced strip and cording, make 1½ yards of corded piping. With right sides facing and raw edges aligned, stitch piping to design piece.

**4.** With right sides facing and raw edges aligned, stitch backing to design piece, sewing along stitching line of piping and leaving an opening for turning. Clip curves and turn. Slipstitch opening closed.

### Stitches to Go On

With your supervision, older children will be delighted to help with the holiday preparations by stenciling the napkins. Treat yourself to an updated hostess apron by stitching these rich fall motifs along the hem.

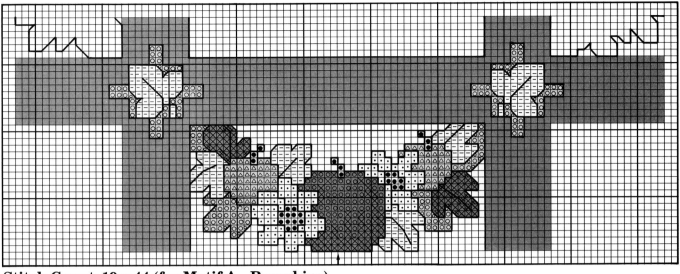

**Stitch Count: 19 x 44 (for Motif A—Pumpkins)**
**14 x 14 (for Motif B—Leaf)**

### SAMPLE for Napkin Ring
Stitched on Vanessa-Ann Afghan Weave 18 over 2 threads, the finished design size is 2⅛" x 4⅞". Stitch Pumpkins only (see graph for placement). The fabric was cut 11" x 11" (finished measurement includes 1 whole block and ¼ block on each side). See page 142 for afghan material.

### MATERIALS (for 1 napkin ring)
Completed cross-stitch on Vanessa-Ann Afghan Weave 18; matching thread
⅛ yard of mustard yellow fabric; matching thread
½ yard (⅛") cording

### DIRECTIONS
All seam allowances are ¼".

**1.** With design centered, trim design piece to 9" wide. Measure and mark ¼" outside top and bottom edges of design. Set aside.

**2.** From mustard yellow fabric, cut 1 (2¾" x 10") piece for backing. From remainder, cut 1"-wide bias strips, piecing as needed to equal ½ yard. Using pieced strip and cording, make ½ yard of corded piping. Cut piping into 2 (9") lengths. With raw edges of 1 length of piping aligned with 1 marked line on design piece and piping toward center, stitch piping to right side of design piece. Trim excess fabric from seam allowance. Repeat to attach remaining length of piping.

**3.** With right sides facing, raw edges aligned, and short edges aligned at 1 end, stitch backing to design piece along long raw edges, sewing along stitching lines of piping. Turn.

**4.** Turn short raw edges of design piece under ¼" and slipstitch ends together, leaving backing unstitched. Turn long unstitched edge of backing under ¼" and slipstitch to backing and piping, covering other end of backing.

| Anchor | | DMC (used for sample) | |
|---|---|---|---|
| **Step 1: Cross-stitch (3 strands)** | | | |
| 891 | · | 676 | Old Gold-lt. |
| 11 | △ | 3328 | Salmon-dk. |
| 5968 | ○ ⬕ | 355 | Terra Cotta-dk. |
| 323 | ◉ | 722 | Orange Spice-lt. |
| 349 | ✕ ◪ | 921 | Copper |
| 363 | – ◿ | 436 | Tan |
| 351 | ● | 400 | Mahogany-dk. |
| **Step 2: Backstitch (1 strand)** | | | |
| 351 | | 400 | Mahogany-dk. |

**Decorative weave of fabric**

## MATERIALS (for 1 napkin)

⅝ yard of mustard yellow fabric; matching thread
Manila folder
Scrap of mat board or cardboard
Drafting tape
Craft knife
Acrylic fabric paints: orange, dark orange, light brown, brown, yellow
Stencil brush
Small paintbrush
Tracing paper

## DIRECTIONS

**1.** Cut 1 (20½") square from mustard yellow fabric. Fold all edges ¼" twice to back and stitch.

**2.** Transfer stencil patterns to tracing paper and cut out. Transfer stencil patterns to manila folder. Using drafting tape, secure folder to mat board. Using craft knife, cut out stencils.

**3.** When stenciling, allow each color to dry before beginning the next. Referring to photograph, stencil designs ½" from hem in the following order: 1 orange pumpkin in center of 1 corner of napkin; then 1 yellow flower on each side of pumpkin. Next stencil brown stem on pumpkin and brown centers on flowers.

Referring to photo and using small paintbrush and light brown paint, lightly paint flower petals out from flower center. Using dark orange paint, lightly paint pumpkin "seams" from stem.

**Stencil Patterns**

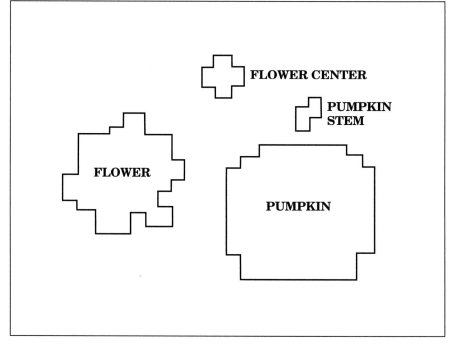

FLOWER CENTER

PUMPKIN STEM

FLOWER

PUMPKIN

**PLACE MAT**

Cut 1 from fused design piece.
Cut 1 from mustard yellow fabric.
Add ¼" seam allowance.

Place on fold.

Place on fold.

## DECEMBER 21
# *First Day of Winter*

*The exhilarating air, newly fallen snow, and sparkling icicles are the real glories of winter. This snowy cross-stitch scene invites you outdoors to enjoy the pleasures of the chilly wonderland.*

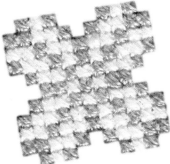

**110**

# Snowflakes

## SAMPLE

Stitched on white Aida 14 over 1 thread, the finished design size is 9¼" x 7⅜". The fabric was cut 16" x 14". See page 140 for framing ideas.

| FABRICS | DESIGN SIZES |
|---|---|
| Aida 11 | 11⅞" x 9⅜" |
| Aida 18 | 7¼" x 5¾" |
| Hardanger 22 | 5⅞" x 4⅝" |

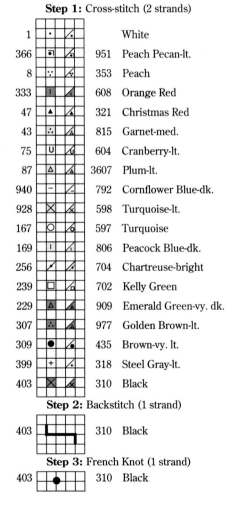

| Anchor | | | DMC | (used for sample) |
|---|---|---|---|---|

**Step 1:** Cross-stitch (2 strands)

| 1 | | | | White |
|---|---|---|---|---|
| 366 | | | 951 | Peach Pecan-lt. |
| 8 | | | 353 | Peach |
| 333 | | | 608 | Orange Red |
| 47 | | | 321 | Christmas Red |
| 43 | | | 815 | Garnet-med. |
| 75 | U | | 604 | Cranberry-lt. |
| 87 | △ | | 3607 | Plum-lt. |
| 940 | – | | 792 | Cornflower Blue-dk. |
| 928 | ✕ | | 598 | Turquoise-lt. |
| 167 | O | | 597 | Turquoise |
| 169 | I | | 806 | Peacock Blue-dk. |
| 256 | ╱ | | 704 | Chartreuse-bright |
| 239 | ☐ | | 702 | Kelly Green |
| 229 | ▲ | | 909 | Emerald Green-vy. dk. |
| 307 | | | 977 | Golden Brown-lt. |
| 309 | ● | | 435 | Brown-vy. lt. |
| 399 | + | | 318 | Steel Gray-lt. |
| 403 | ✕ | | 310 | Black |

**Step 2:** Backstitch (1 strand)

| 403 | | 310 | Black |
|---|---|---|---|

**Step 3:** French Knot (1 strand)

| 403 | ● | 310 | Black |
|---|---|---|---|

**Stitch Count: 130 x 103**

113

# Christmas Eve

*Salute the diverse cultures that have shaped our
own holiday traditions with this spirited trio of designs.
Express your fondness for rousing colors with the flag-
waving Santa stocking at left. Bind the Scandinavian
tree skirt and stocking (pages 120 and 124) in
the charm of a warm country plaid.*

## Santa Stocking

### SAMPLE
Stitched on white Aida 14 over
1 thread, the finished design
size is 11⅜" x 15⅞". The fabric
was cut 18" x 22". See page 142
for Balger braid.

### FABRICS

| FABRICS | DESIGN SIZES |
|---|---|
| Aida 11 | 14½" x 20¼" |
| Aida 18 | 8⅞" x 12⅜" |
| Hardanger 22 | 7¼" x 10⅛" |

### MATERIALS
Completed cross-stitch on
   white Aida 14
1 yard of coordinating print
   fabric; matching thread
¼ yard of red fabric
1¼ yards (¼") cording

### DIRECTIONS
All seam allowances are ¼".

**1.** Trim design piece to ¼"
outside of stitched area.

**2.** Using design piece as pattern and with wrong sides facing, cut 1 stocking piece from
print fabric for back. With right
sides facing, fold remaining
print fabric in half. Cutting
through both layers, cut 2
stocking pieces for lining. From
red fabric, cut 1 (1½" x 4½")
strip. From remainder, cut 1¼"-
wide bias strips, piecing as
needed to equal 42".

**3.** Using pieced red strip and
cording, make 42" of corded
piping. With right sides facing
and raw edges aligned, stitch
piping around sides and bottom
of design piece.

**4.** For hanger, with right
sides facing and raw edges
aligned, fold 1½" x 4½" red
strip in half lengthwise. Stitch
long raw edges together. Turn.
Center seam and press. Fold
hanger piece in half to make a
loop. With right sides facing,
raw edges aligned, and loop
toward center, pin hanger to
top right edge of back.

**5.** With right sides facing
and raw edges aligned, stitch
stocking back to design piece,
sewing along stitching line of
piping and leaving top open.
Clip curves and turn.

**6.** To make lining, with right
sides facing and raw edges
aligned, stitch lining pieces
together, leaving top edge open
and large opening in side seam
above heel. Clip curves but do
not turn. With right sides facing, slide lining over stocking,
matching side seams. With raw
edges aligned, stitch around
top edge of stocking, securing
hanger in seam. Turn through
opening in lining. Slipstitch
opening closed. Tuck lining
inside stocking.

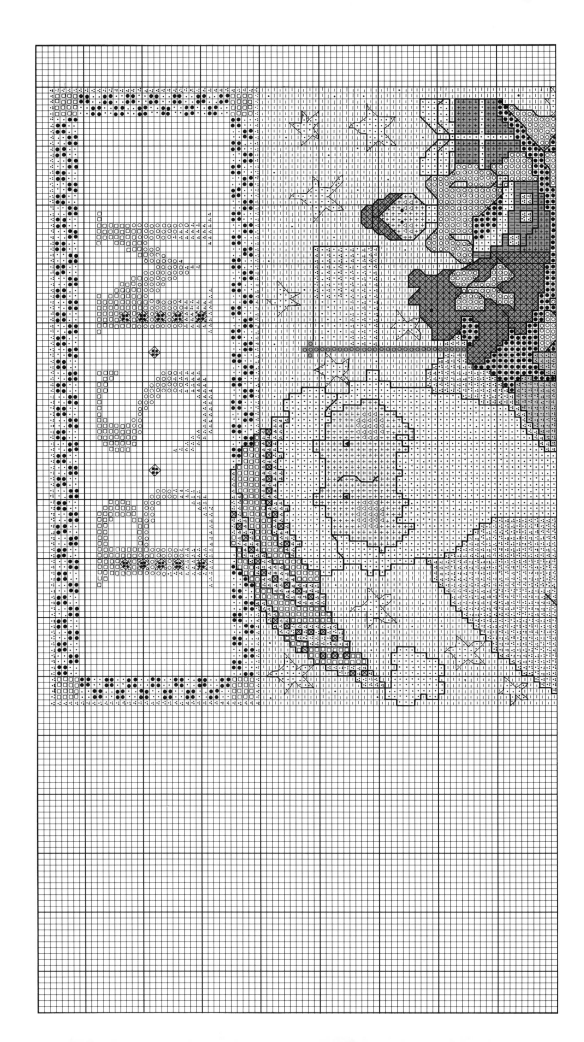

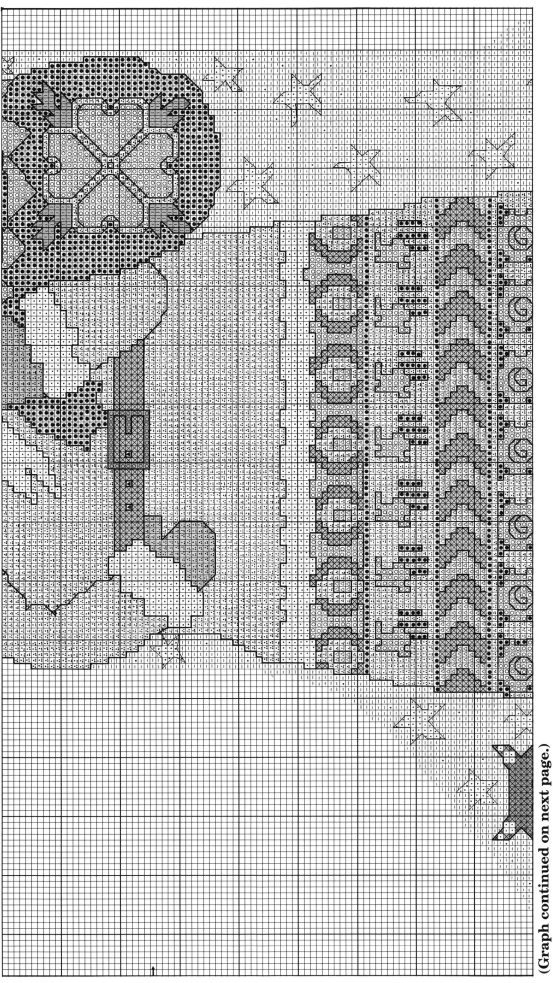

**(Graph continued on next page.)**

**117**

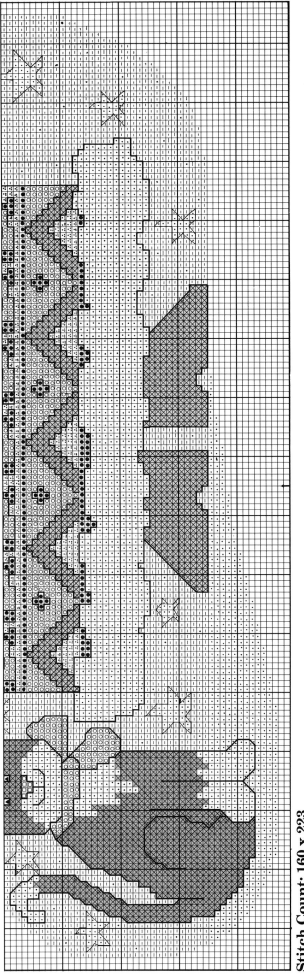

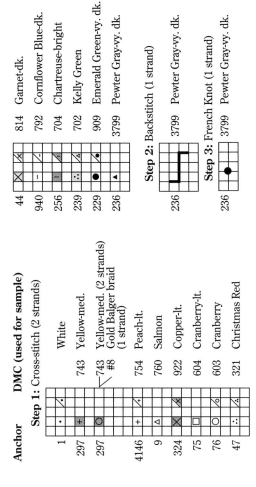

**Stitch Count: 160 x 223**

| Anchor | DMC (used for sample) | | | | | | | | |
|---|---|---|---|---|---|---|---|---|---|
| **Step 1: Cross-stitch (2 strands)** | | | | | | | | | |
| 1 | · | White | | | | | | | |
| 297 | + | 743 | Yellow-med. | | | | | | |
| 297 | O | 743 #8 | Yellow-med. (2 strands) Gold Balger braid (1 strand) | | | | | | |
| 4146 | + | 754 | Peach-lt. | | | | | | |
| 9 | △ | 760 | Salmon | | | | | | |
| 324 | X | 922 | Copper-lt. | | | | | | |
| 75 | □ | 604 | Cranberry-lt. | | | | | | |
| 76 | ⊘ | 603 | Cranberry | | | | | | |
| 47 | ∴ | 321 | Christmas Red | | | | | | |

| Anchor | | DMC | | | | | | | |
|---|---|---|---|---|---|---|---|---|---|
| 44 | X | 814 | Garnet-dk. | | | | | | |
| 940 | – | 792 | Cornflower Blue-dk. | | | | | | |
| 256 | ⊿ | 704 | Chartreuse-bright | | | | | | |
| 239 | ∴ | 702 | Kelly Green | | | | | | |
| 229 | ● | 909 | Emerald Green-vy. dk. | | | | | | |
| 236 | ▲ | 3799 | Pewter Gray-vy. dk. | | | | | | |

**Step 2: Backstitch (1 strand)**

| 236 | | 3799 | Pewter Gray-vy. dk. |
|---|---|---|---|

**Step 3: French Knot (1 strand)**

| 236 | ● | 3799 | Pewter Gray-vy. dk. |
|---|---|---|---|

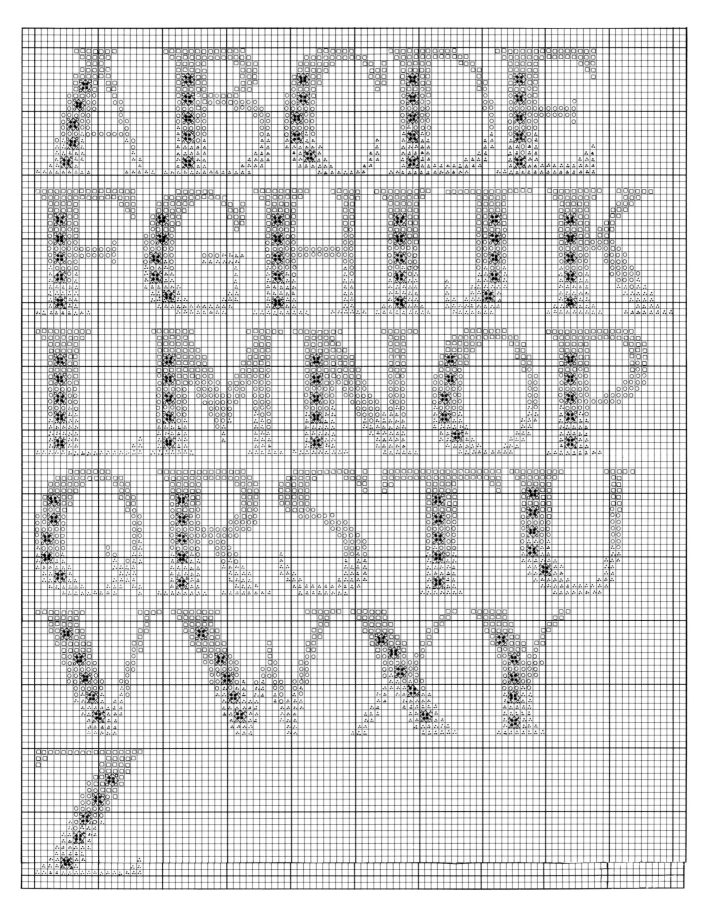

119

# Scandinavian Tree Skirt

## SAMPLE
Stitched on beige Klostern 7 over 1 thread, the finished design size is 37⅛" x 11⅜" for 1 repeat. The fabric was cut 62" x 62". Beginning 3" from 1 edge, stitch 1 repeat along each side, omitting zigzag motif on 1 side to allow for slit placement (see Diagram).

| FABRICS | DESIGN SIZES |
|---|---|
| Aida 11 | 23⅝" x 7¼" |
| Aida 14 | 18⅝" x 5¾" |
| Aida 18 | 14½" x 4½" |
| Hardanger 22 | 11⅞" x 3⅝" |

## MATERIALS
Completed cross-stitch on beige
  Klostern 7; matching thread
1 yard of red plaid fabric
11 (⅝") dark gray buttons
Dressmaker's pen

## DIRECTIONS
All seam allowances are ¼".

**1.** With design centered and outside row of stitches 1½" from each edge, trim design piece to 51" x 51". From red plaid fabric, cut 1¾"-wide bias strips, piecing as needed to equal 7¾ yards. Referring to graph for placement, stitch buttons to design piece.

**2.** Fold design piece into fourths and mark center. Unfold. Mark 6"-diameter circle around center and cut out. Cut slit from circle through center of unstitched edge (see Diagram).

**3.** To bind edges, with right sides facing and raw edges aligned, stitch bias strip to design piece, mitering corners and easing strip along center circle. Double-fold strip to wrong side, making ⅝"-wide self binding. Slipstitch in place over stitching line.

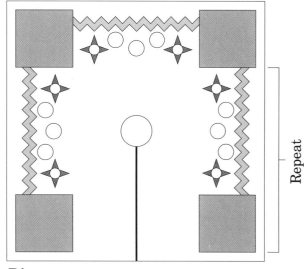

**Diagram**

Repeat

**Stitch Count: 260 x 80 (for 1 repeat)**

**Right side**

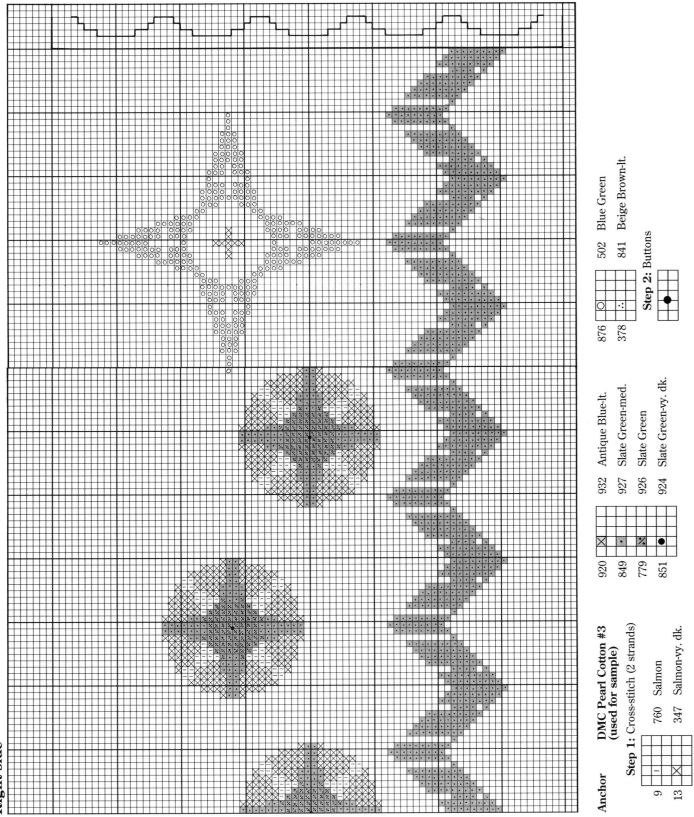

Anchor    **DMC Pearl Cotton #3**
            **(used for sample)**

**Step 1:** Cross-stitch (2 strands)

| | |
|---|---|
| 9 | 760   Salmon |
| 13 | 347   Salmon-vy. dk. |

| | | | | |
|---|---|---|---|---|
| 920 | ⊠ | | | Antique Blue-lt. |
| 849 | | ∴ | | Slate Green-med. |
| 779 | | | ⊠ | Slate Green |
| 851 | | | ● | Slate Green-vy. dk. |

| | | | |
|---|---|---|---|
| 876 | ○ | | Blue Green |
| 378 | ∴ | | Beige Brown-lt. |

**Step 2:** Buttons

●

**123**

# Scandinavian Stocking

**SAMPLE**
Stitched on beige Tula 10 over 1 thread, the finished design size is 9¾" x 14¾". The fabric was cut 14" x 18".

| FABRICS | DESIGN SIZES |
|---|---|
| Aida 11 | 8⅞" x 13⅜" |
| Aida 14 | 7" x 10½" |
| Aida 18 | 5½" x 8⅛" |
| Hardanger 22 | 4½" x 6⅝" |

**MATERIALS**
Completed cross-stitch on beige
    Tula 10; matching thread
1 (10½" x 15") piece of
    unstitched beige Tula 10
⅜ yard of green plaid fabric
¼ yard of red plaid fabric
⅜ yard of fleece
1¼ yards (¼") cording
7 (⅝") dark gray buttons
Tracing paper
Dressmaker's pen

**DIRECTIONS**
All seam allowances are ¼".

**1.** Transfer stocking outline to tracing paper, adding seam allowance. Center pattern on design piece and cut out. From unstitched Tula, cut 1 stocking piece for back. With right sides facing, fold green plaid fabric in half. Cutting through both layers, cut 2 stocking pieces for lining, adding 3¾" at top. From remainder, cut 2 (8" x 3¾") bias strips for stocking top and 1 (1¼" x 4") strip for hanger. From fleece, cut 2 stocking pieces, adding 3¾" at top. From red plaid fabric, cut 2"-wide bias strips, piecing as needed to equal 1¼ yards. Using pieced strip and cording, make 1¼ yards of corded piping.

**2.** Referring to graph for placement, stitch buttons to design piece.

**3.** For stocking front, with right sides facing and raw edges aligned, stitch 1 long edge of 1 green plaid bias strip to top edge of design piece. Pin 1 fleece piece to wrong side of stocking front. Repeat to make stocking back. With right sides facing and raw edges aligned, stitch piping around sides and bottom of stocking front.

**4.** For hanger, with right sides facing and raw edges aligned, fold hanger strip in half lengthwise. Stitch long raw edges together. Turn. Center seam and press. Fold hanger piece in half to make a loop. With right sides facing, raw edges aligned, and loop toward center, pin hanger to top right edge of back.

**5.** With right sides facing and raw edges aligned, stitch stocking front to back, sewing along stitching line of piping and leaving top open. Trim fleece from seam allowance. Clip curves and turn.

**6.** To make lining, with right sides facing and raw edges aligned, stitch lining pieces together, leaving top edge open and large opening in side seam above heel. Clip curves but do not turn. With right sides facing, slide lining over stocking, matching side seams. With raw edges aligned, stitch around top edge of stocking, securing hanger in seam. Turn through opening in lining. Slipstitch opening closed. Tuck lining inside stocking.

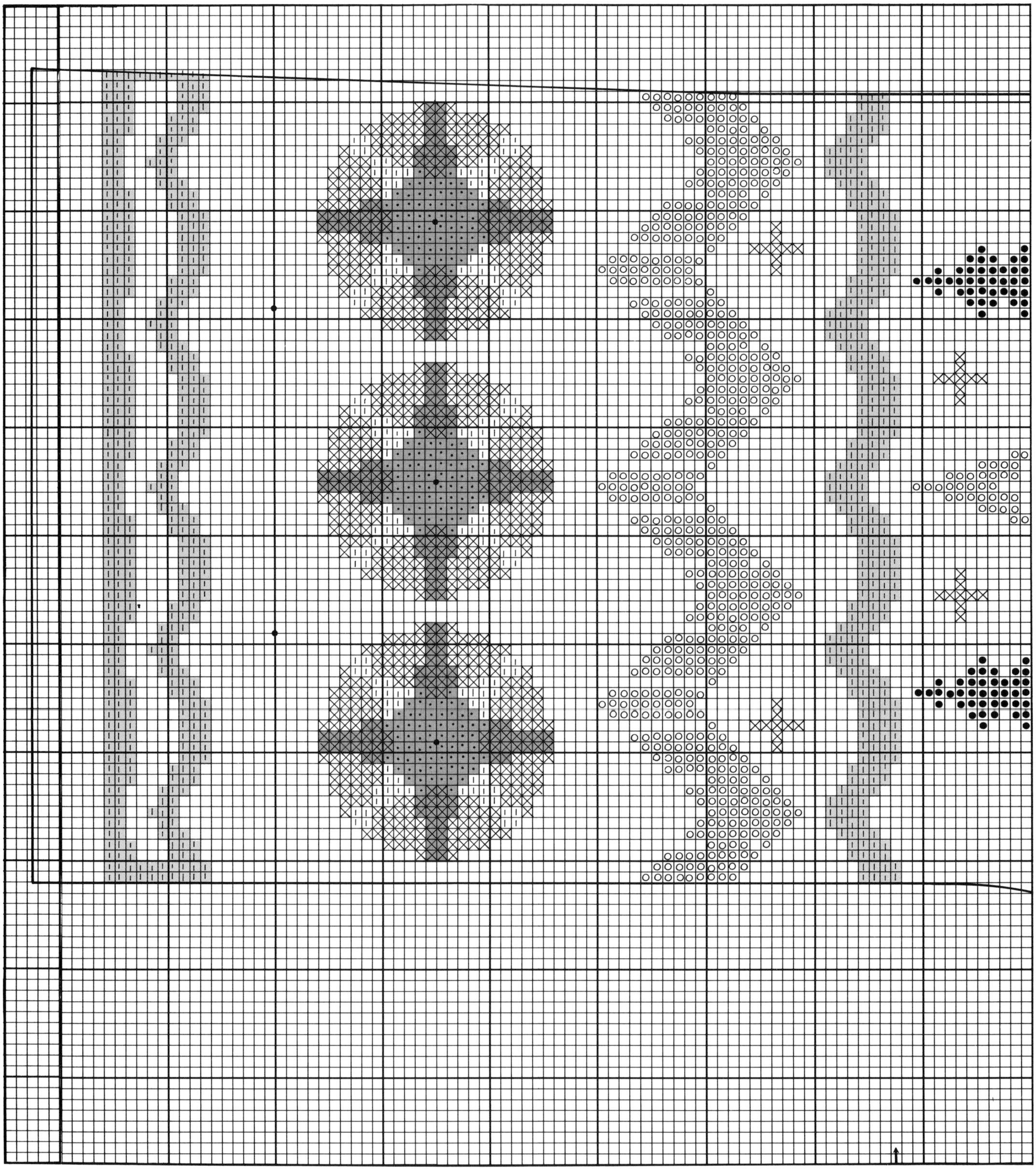

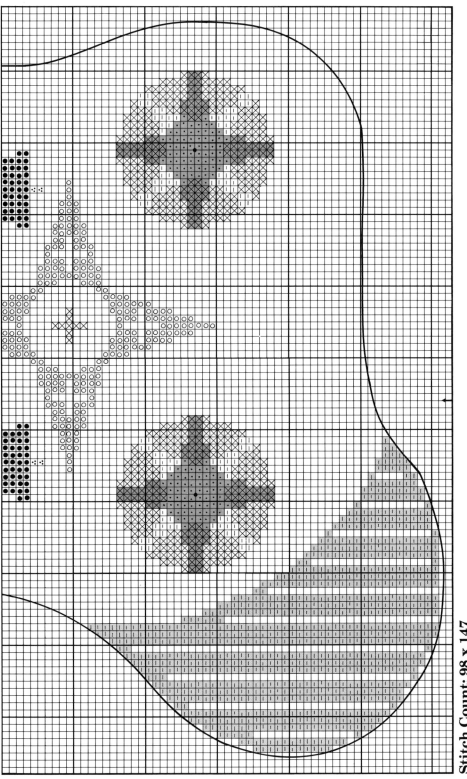

**Stitch Count: 98 x 147**

Anchor | DMC Pearl Cotton #5 (used for sample)

**Step 1:** Cross-stitch (1 strand)

| | | |
|---|---|---|
| 9 | − | 760 Salmon |
| 13 | ✕ | 347 Salmon-vy. dk. |
| 900 | · | 928 Slate Green-lt. |
| 851 | ● | 924 Slate Green-vy. dk. |
| 876 | ○ | 502 Blue Green |

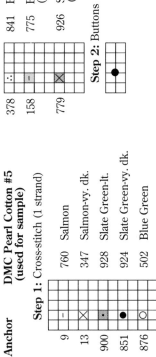

| | | |
|---|---|---|
| 378 | ∴ | 841 Beige Brown-lt. |
| 158 | − | 775 Baby Blue-vy. lt. (DMC floss, 3 strands) |
| 779 | ✕ | 926 Slate Green (DMC floss, 3 strands) |

**Step 2:** Buttons

**127**

# Christmas Day

*Celebrate the height of the holiday stitching season with a pair of special projects. In time you can expect the loving portrait of Santa at left to become an heirloom. Express your happiest Christmas sentiments with the playful sweatshirt shown on page 135.*

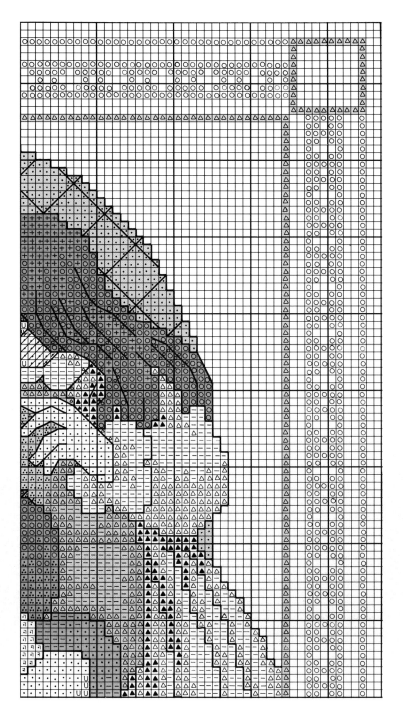

# Santa Claus

## SAMPLE

Stitched on white Belfast Linen 32 over 2 threads, the finished design size is 8¼" x 10¾". The fabric was cut 15" x 17". See page 142 for Balger blending filament.

| FABRICS | DESIGN SIZES |
|---|---|
| Aida 11 | 11⅞" x 15¾" |
| Aida 14 | 9⅜" x 12⅜" |
| Aida 18 | 7¼" x 9⅝" |
| Hardanger 22 | 6" x 7⅞" |

| Anchor | | | DMC (used for sample) |
|---|---|---|---|

**Step 1:** Cross-stitch (2 strands)

| Anchor | | | DMC | |
|---|---|---|---|---|
| 1 | · | ⁄ | | White |
| 386 | ▫ | ▫ | 746 | Off White |
| 886 | ∴ | ⁄ | 677 | Old Gold-vy. lt. |
| 891 | + | ⁄ | 676 | Old Gold-lt. |
| 890 | O | ⁄ | 729 | Old Gold-med. |
| 880 | · | ⁄ | 754 | Peach-lt. |
| 4146 | U | ⁄ | 950 | Peach Pecan-dk. |
| 882 | ⁄ | ⁄ | 3773 | Pecan-vy. lt. |
| 8 | + | ⁄ | 761 | Salmon-lt. |
| 13 | – | ⁄ | 347 | Salmon-vy. dk. |
| 13 | △ | ⁄ | 347 | Salmon-vy. dk. (1 strand) |
| 897 | | | 221 | Shell Pink-vy. dk. (1 strand) |
| 897 | ∴ | ⁄ | 221 | Shell Pink-vy. dk. |
| 968 | – | ⁄ | 316 | Antique Mauve-med. |
| 969 | △ | ⁄ | 3726 | Antique Mauve-dk. |
| 970 | ▲ | ⁄ | 315 | Antique Mauve-vy. dk. |
| 975 | ◇ | ⁄ | 3753 | Antique Blue-ultra vy. lt. |

Color code continued on page 133.

**Lower half**

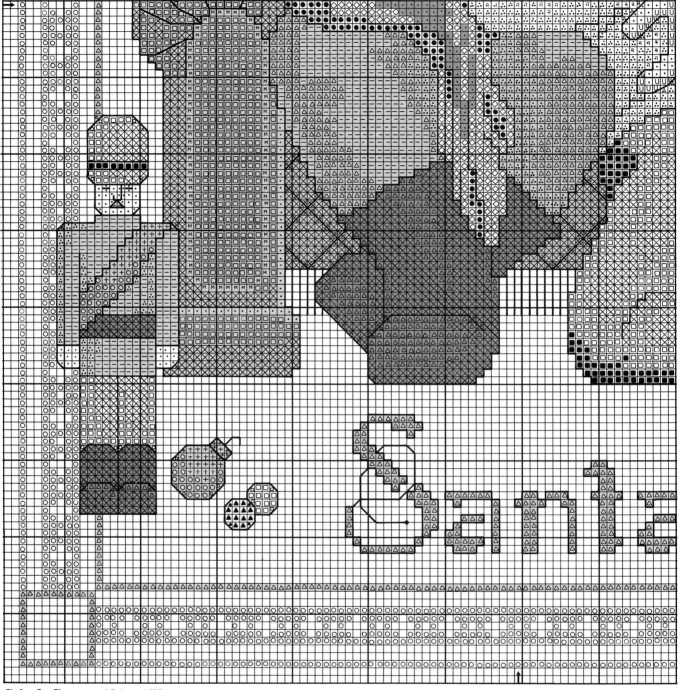

**Stitch Count: 131 x 173**

| | | | | | |
|---|---|---|---|---|---|
| 343 | ● | ◢ | 3752 | Antique Blue-vy. lt. |
| 920 | ✕ | ◢ | 932 | Antique Blue-lt. |
| 921 | □ | ◢ | 931 | Antique Blue-med. |
| 922 | ■ | ◢ | 930 | Antique Blue-dk. |
| 849 | ○ | | 927 | Slate Green-med. |
| 210 | · | ◢ | 562 | Jade-med. |
| 878 | □ | ◢ | 501 | Blue Green-dk. |
| 879 | ✕ | ◢ | 500 | Blue Green-vy. dk. |
| 362 | + | | 437 | Tan-lt. |
| 309 | ○ | ◢ | 435 | Brown-vy. lt. |
| 371 | ⋰ | ◢ | 433 | Brown-med. |
| 398 | ▨ | ◢ | 415 | Pearl Gray |
| 399 | □ | ◢ | 318 | Steel Gray-lt. |
| 400 | △ | ◢ | 414 | Steel Gray-dk. |
| 236 | ✕ | ◢ | 3799 | Pewter Gray-vy. dk. |
| | M | | 085 | Peacock Balger blending filament (2 strands) |

**Step 2:** Backstitch (1 strand)

| | | | |
|---|---|---|---|
| 897 | | 221 | Shell Pink-vy. dk. (lettering) |
| 72 | | 902 | Garnet-vy. dk. (girl's dress) |
| 371 | | 433 | Brown-med. (faces, hands, feet, girl's and baby's hair, horn, rattle, gold ornaments) |
| 236 | | 3799 | Pewter Gray-vy. dk. (all else) |
| | | 085 | Peacock Balger blending filament (chair weave) |

**Step 3:** Long Stitch (2 strands)

| | | |
|---|---|---|
| | 085 | Peacock Balger blending filament (chair fringe) |

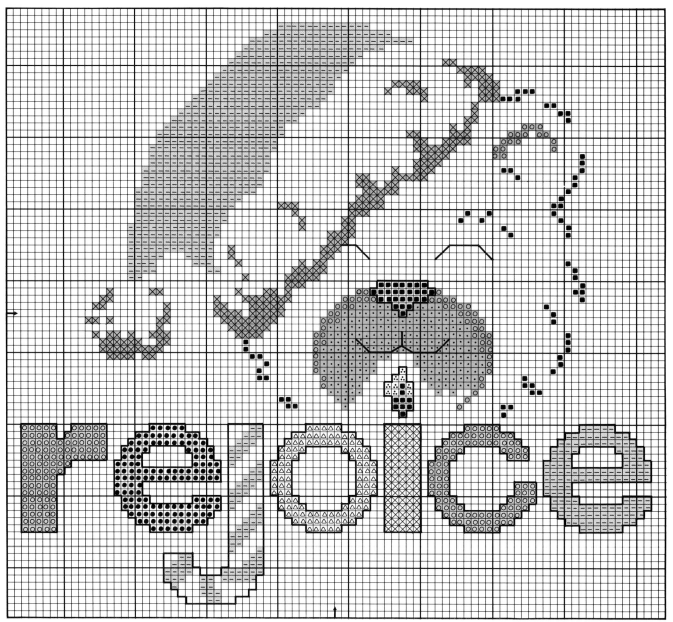

**Stitch Count: 88 x 81**

# Rejoice
# Sweatshirt

### SAMPLE

Stitched with Waste Canvas 10 on purchased white sweat-shirt, the finished design size is 8⅛" x 8⅛". The canvas was cut 10" x 10". See page 137 for working with waste canvas.

### FABRICS        DESIGN SIZES
Aida 11          8" x 7⅜"
Aida 14          6¼" x 5¾"
Aida 18          4⅞" x 4½"
Hardanger 22     4" x 3⅝"

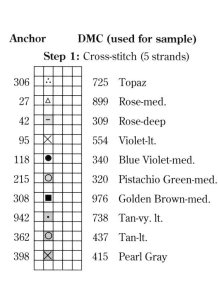

| Anchor | | DMC (used for sample) | |
|---|---|---|---|
| | | **Step 1: Cross-stitch (5 strands)** | |
| 306 | ∴ | 725 | Topaz |
| 27 | △ | 899 | Rose-med. |
| 42 | − | 309 | Rose-deep |
| 95 | ✕ | 554 | Violet-lt. |
| 118 | ● | 340 | Blue Violet-med. |
| 215 | ○ | 320 | Pistachio Green-med. |
| 308 | ■ | 976 | Golden Brown-med. |
| 942 | · | 738 | Tan-vy. lt. |
| 362 | ◯ | 437 | Tan-lt. |
| 398 | ✕ | 415 | Pearl Gray |

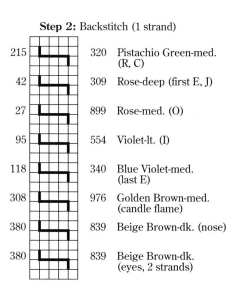

| Anchor | | **Step 2: Backstitch (1 strand)** | |
|---|---|---|---|
| 215 | | 320 | Pistachio Green-med. (R, C) |
| 42 | | 309 | Rose-deep (first E, J) |
| 27 | | 899 | Rose-med. (O) |
| 95 | | 554 | Violet-lt. (I) |
| 118 | | 340 | Blue Violet-med. (last E) |
| 308 | | 976 | Golden Brown-med. (candle flame) |
| 380 | | 839 | Beige Brown-dk. (nose) |
| 380 | | 839 | Beige Brown-dk. (eyes, 2 strands) |

# General Instructions

## CROSS-STITCH

**Fabrics:** Most designs in this book are worked on even-weave fabrics that are made especially for cross-stitch and can be found in your local needlework shop. If you cannot find a fabric, see Suppliers on page 142 for ordering information.

Fabrics used in models are identified in sample information by color, name, and thread count per inch.

**Finished Design Size:** Finished design sizes are given for 11-, 14-, 18-, and 22-count fabrics. To determine size of finished design, divide stitch count by number of threads per inch of fabric. When design is stitched over 2 threads, divide stitch count by half the number of threads per inch.

**Preparing Fabric:** Cut fabric at least 3" larger on all sides than finished design size to ensure enough space for matting, framing, and other finishing techniques. To prevent fraying, whipstitch, machine-zigzag, or apply liquid ravel preventer to raw fabric edges.

*page 60*

**Needles:** Choose a blunt-tipped tapestry needle that will slip easily through fabric holes without piercing fabric threads.

For fabric with 11 or fewer threads per inch, use needle size 24; for 14 threads per inch, use size 24 or 26; and for 18 or more threads per inch, use size 26. Never leave needle in design area of fabric—it may leave rust or a permanent impression on fabric.

**Hoop or Frame:** Using a hoop or stretcher bar frame keeps fabric taut and makes it easier to make uniform stitches.

Select a hoop or frame large enough to hold entire design. Place screw or clamp of hoop in 10 o'clock position (or 2 o'clock if you are left-handed) to keep it from catching floss.

**Graphs and Color Codes:** On graphs, a square containing a symbol represents 1 stitch to be worked. Each symbol corresponds to a specific color of embroidery floss, identified by name and number on color code. Flosses are cross-referenced, giving both DMC and Anchor color numbers.

Color codes indicate stitches to be used and number of floss strands for each stitch. Stitch count for entire design is listed below each graph. Heavy lines on graphs indicate repeats.

**Centering Design:** To find center of fabric, fold it in half horizontally and then vertically. Place pin in intersection of folds to mark center. To find center of graph, follow vertical and horizontal arrows until they intersect. Begin stitching center of design in center of fabric (unless otherwise indicated).

**Embroidery Floss:** Use 18" lengths of floss (longer pieces tend to twist and knot). Dampen floss with wet sponge to straighten. Separate all 6 strands; then recombine number of strands called for in color code. Floss covers best when lying flat. If floss begins to twist, suspend needle and allow floss to unwind.

**Securing Floss:** Bring needle and floss up through fabric, leaving 1" tail on underside. Secure floss tail with first few stitches.

Another method for securing floss is the waste knot. Knot floss and bring needle down through fabric about 1" from where first stitch will be taken. Secure floss on back of fabric with first 4 or 5 stitches. After floss is secured, cut off knot from underside of fabric.

To secure floss after stitching is complete, run needle under 4 or 5 stitches on back of design and clip ends close to fabric.

**Stitching Method:** For smooth stitches, use the push-and-pull method. Starting on wrong side of fabric, bring needle straight up, pulling floss completely through to right side. Reinsert needle and bring it straight down, pulling needle and floss completely through to back of fabric. Keep floss flat but do not pull tight. For even stitches, keep tension consistent throughout.

**Carrying Floss:** To carry floss, weave it under previously worked stitches on back. Do not carry floss across any fabric that is not or will not be stitched. Loose strands, especially dark ones, will show through the fabric.

**Cleaning Completed Work:** When stitching is complete, soak finished piece in cold water with mild soap for 5 to 10 minutes; rinse thoroughly. Roll work in towel to remove excess water; do not wring. Place work face down on dry towel and press with warm iron until work is dry.

*Note:* If design piece includes metallic threads or blending filaments, place a clean, dry cloth between fabric and iron. Press gently.

## WASTE CANVAS

Waste canvas is a coarse fabric used as a guide for cross-stitching on fabrics other than even weaves. Cut waste canvas at least 1" larger on all sides than finished design size. Baste waste canvas to fabric to be stitched. Each stitch is over 1 unit (2 threads).

When stitching is complete, use spray bottle to dampen stitched area with cold water. Using tweezers, pull out waste canvas threads 1 at a time; pull out all threads running in 1 direction first; then pull out opposite threads. Let stitching dry. Then place face down on towel; iron.

## PERFORATED PAPER

Cut perforated paper at least 1" larger on all sides than finished design size. Stitch over 1  space (see left). Be careful when pulling thread; too much tension can tear the small spaces between perforations. When stitching is complete, trim paper to 1 hole outside design, being careful not to cut into any hole holding a stitch.

### STITCHES TO GO ON

We have included this handy tip box to give you ideas for creating additional projects from the original designs. Explore these boxes for easy gift ideas.

*page 26*

## COMMON STITCHES

**Cross-stitch:** Make 1 cross for each symbol on graph. Bring needle up at A, down at B, up at C, and down at D (Diagram 1). For horizontal rows, stitch from left to right to make half-crosses and then back to complete stitches (Diagram 2). For vertical rows, complete each stitch individually. All stitches should lie in same direction—all understitches must slant in 1 direction and all overstitches must slant in opposite direction.

**Diagram 1**

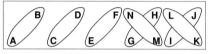

**Diagram 2**

**Three-quarter Stitch:** Three-quarter stitch is used to make a curved line. It is indicated on graph when symbol fills only half of square (Diagram 3). If you are working over 1 thread, short understitch will pierce fabric thread; if you are working over 2 threads, it will slip through hole between 2 threads. Make long stitch in direction of slanted line on graph. Long stitch is always overstitch.

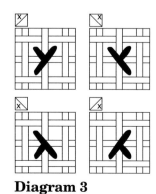

**Diagram 3**

When 2 symbols occupy single square on graph, make a three-quarter stitch and a quarter stitch to fill square. Which symbol applies to which stitch depends on line you want to emphasize. Use three-quarter stitch to express dominant line or color (Diagram 4).

**Diagram 4**

**Backstitch:** Complete all cross-stitches before working backstitches or other accent stitches. Working from right to left with 1 strand of floss (unless otherwise indicated), bring needle up at A, down at B, and up at C (Diagram 5). Going back down at A, continue in this manner.

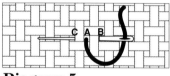

**Diagram 5**

**French Knot:** Bring needle up at A. Wrap floss around needle twice (unless otherwise indicated). Insert needle beside A, pulling floss until it fits snugly around needle. Pull needle through to back (Diagram 6).

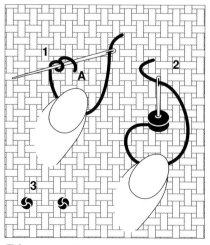

**Diagram 6**

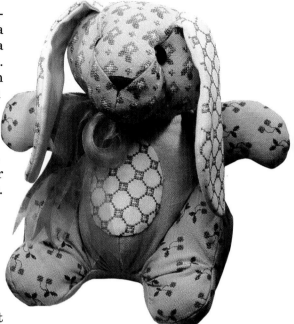

*page 36*

## SEWING HINTS

**Bias Strips:** In this book, bias strips are used to make corded piping and corded tubing. To cut bias strips, fold fabric at 45° angle to grain of fabric and crease. Cut along crease. Cut strips to measure width indicated in directions, cutting parallel to first cutting line. Ends of bias strips should be cut on grain of fabric. With right sides facing, place ends of strips together as shown and stitch with ¼" seam (Diagram 7). Continue to piece strips until they are length indicated in directions.

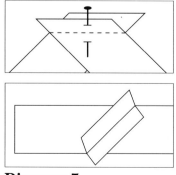

**Diagram 7**

**Corded Piping:** From pieced bias strip and cording, cut length indicated in directions. With wrong sides facing and raw edges aligned, fold pieced strip in half lengthwise, encasing cording in fold. Stitch close to cord to secure.

**Corded Tubing:** From pieced bias strip and cording, cut length indicated in directions. With right sides facing and raw edges aligned, fold pieced strip in half lengthwise. Stitch long raw edges together to make a tube. Turn. Using bodkin, draw cording through tube.

**Gathering and Shirring:** Machine-stitch 2 parallel rows of long stitches ¼" and ½" from raw edge of fabric. Leave thread ends at least 3" long. Pull bobbin threads and gather to fit to desired length. Disperse fullness evenly and secure threads.

**Marking on Fabric:** Always use dressmaker's pen or chalk to mark on fabric. It will wash out when finished piece is cleaned.

**Slipstitch:** The slipstitch is an almost invisible stitch. Use it to secure folded edges of fabric together or folded edge to base fabric (Diagram 8).

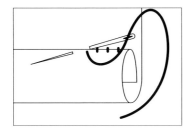

**Diagram 8**

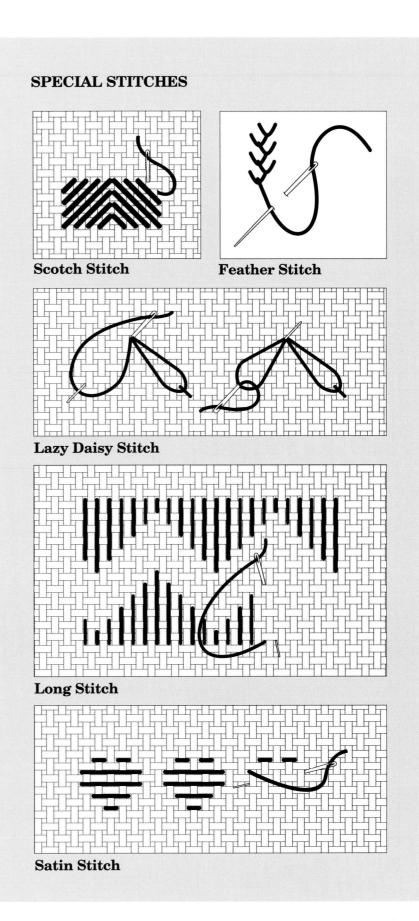

**SPECIAL STITCHES**

**Scotch Stitch**

**Feather Stitch**

**Lazy Daisy Stitch**

**Long Stitch**

**Satin Stitch**

# Framing Ideas

Once you have completed your cross-stitch piece, it is important to find a mat and a frame that will enhance its beauty without overpowering it. These are our professional secrets for perfect results.

## PREPARE DESIGN PIECE

Lacing is the process of mounting your design piece on mat board with strong thread; it is the best way to prepare your design piece for framing. Better frame shops will lace needlework, but it is often quite expensive.

To lace the design piece yourself, you will need the following tools and materials:

Completed cross-stitch piece
2 pieces of paper (at least size of design piece)

Straight pins
White mat board or foam-core board for backing
Ruler
Craft knife
Liquid ravel preventer
Sewing needle and thread
Large-eyed blunt needle
Spool of carpet thread

**1.** Clean, dry, and press design piece (see General Instructions).

**2.** To decide how much fabric should show around design, create a temporary mat. Place design piece right side up on clean surface. Referring to Diagram 1: Cut 2 right angles from paper. Use these to frame design piece until satisfied with effect. Before removing paper, mark position of temporary mat window with pins. Measure and mark with pins desired width of mat. Cut mat-board backing to fit overall size of mat. Remove mat window pins.

**3.** Referring to Diagram 2: Place design piece right side down. Align backing edges with pins. Remove top pin and fold excess fabric over top edge of backing. Following a horizontal thread, push pins ½" apart through fabric into edge of backing. Leave corners loose. Repeat with bottom, left, and right edges, keeping tension even all around. Do not pull fabric so taut that backing bends or fabric weave is distorted. Trim fabric, leaving 2" margin all around. Apply liquid ravel preventer to edges of fabric and let dry.

**4.** Miter each corner; pin (Diagram 3). Working on 1 side at a time, remove pins from edge of backing and push them into edge of fabric at a 45° angle, keeping fabric taut (Diagram 4). Beginning in outer corner, stitch each mitered corner together (Diagram 5).

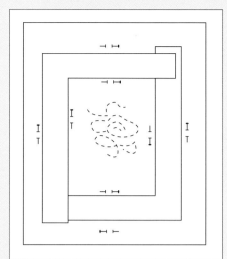

**Diagram 1**
Mark temporary mat window.

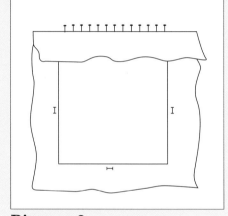

**Diagram 2**
Pin fabric to edge of backing.

Remove all remaining pins.

**5.** Draw a guideline ⅝" from raw edges of fabric. Thread a large-eyed needle from spool of carpet thread; do not cut or knot thread. Referring to Diagram 6: Begin in right corner of top margin and draw thread down through fabric at guideline. (Do not pierce fabric; insert needle between threads.) Draw thread up through bottom margin and down again through top margin, following a horizontal thread. Continue lacing along top and bottom margins until complete.

Cut off needle and knot thread to secure but leave thread attached to spool. Working backward toward spool, pull each lacing taut

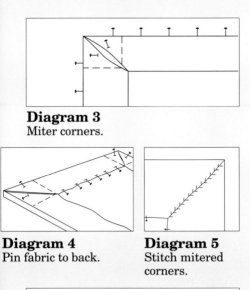

**Diagram 3**
Miter corners.

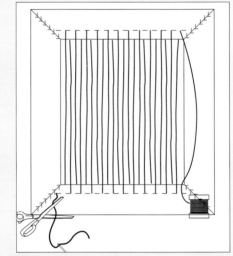

**Diagram 4**
Pin fabric to back.

**Diagram 5**
Stitch mitered corners.

**Diagram 6**
Lace design piece.

without distorting fabric weave or causing backing to bow. Cut thread from spool; secure. Repeat to lace fabric from side to side.

## DECORATIVE MATS

The color and texture of a mat should complement the piece without detracting from it. As a general rule, designs should be matted with equal unstitched space at top and sides, with ⅛" to ½" extra space at bottom. This prevents piece from looking top-heavy. Have a professional cut your mat, as cutting your own can be difficult. After mat is cut, customize it for your cross-stitch piece.

• Layer 2 or more mats in contrasting colors and graduated sizes (see pages 77 and 83). If desired, when using 2 mats, have framer cut designs out of top mat (see page 45).

• Glue cardboard spacers between mats for a shadow-box effect. You will need a box-type frame to accommodate extra depth.

• Draw designs on mat with markers or colored pencils. See page 111 where colored pencils were used to enhance tones in cross-stitch. For festive accents, try metallic inks. You will find stencils are helpful for creating precise shapes.

• Splatter-paint mat with acrylic paints (see page 23). Dilute paint with water. Dab an old toothbrush in paint and pull your finger or a blunt knife across bristles to splatter.

• Glue fabric to mat for textural interest (see page 73). Coat mat with spray adhesive and smooth fabric onto it. Cut fabric, leaving ¼" to ½" margin inside mat window and outside edges. Clip corners; fold fabric to back and glue.

• Cover mat with paper doilies or lace for a charming Victorian effect (see page 27).

## CREATIVE FRAMES

The frame is the finishing touch for your design piece. So that textures can be seen clearly, cross-stitch is often framed without a sheet of glass. If you do use glass, do not let it touch design piece or it will flatten stitches.

Wooden frames go well with cross-stitch and are most suitable for creative customizing. Look for interesting frames at garage sales and secondhand stores. Here are several ideas for embellishing your frame:

• Paint unfinished frame with acrylic paints or spray paint. For glossier look, coat frame with an acrylic gloss finish.

• Decorate with random patterns such as dots or stripes. See page 110 where small, painted dots imitate snowflakes in piece. Or pull motifs from design piece, such as on page 18 where carrots were painted freehand on frame.

• Splatter- or sponge-paint frame. To splatter-paint, see Decorative Mats above. To sponge-paint, do not dilute paint. Dip small, slightly damp sponge into paint; squeeze out excess. Dab sponge randomly on frame. If desired, layer various colors.

• Stencil designs on frame. Choose patterns to complement theme of design, such as Fourth of July stars on page 80. Transfer desired design onto heavy paper and cut out with craft knife. Tape stencil to surface; then paint.

• Glue purchased wooden cutouts to frame. On page 12, motifs were painted on frame after cutouts were attached. Also see page 23 where painted cutouts were glued inside frame window.

# Suppliers

All products are available retail from Shepherd's Bush, 220 24th Street, Ogden, UT 84401; (801) 399-4546. To find a merchant near you, write or call the following suppliers:

## FABRICS

### Chapelle Fabrics
Chapelle Ltd.
P.O. Box 9252
Newgate Station
Ogden, UT 84409
(801) 621-2777

Vanessa-Ann Afghan Weave 18

### Charles Craft Fabrics
Charles Craft
P.O. Box 1049
Laurinburg, NC 28353
(800) 277-0980

Natural Linen 36
Waste Canvas 10
Waste Canvas 14

### Wichelt Fabrics
Wichelt Imports, Inc.
Rural Route 1
Stoddard, WI 54658
(608) 788-4600

Amber Linen 28
Light Blue Jobelan 28
White Jobelan 28

### Zweigart Fabrics
Zweigart/Joan Toggitt Ltd.
Weston Canal Plaza
2 Riverview Drive
Somerset, NJ 08873
(908) 271-1949

Amaretto Murano 30
Antique Green Hardanger 22
Ash Rose Annabelle 28
Beige Klostern 7
Beige Tula 10
Carnation Pastel Linen 28
Carnation Pink Damask
    Aida 14
Cream Aida 14
Cream Aida 18
Cream Hardanger 22
Dirty Linen Dublin Linen 25
Driftwood Belfast Linen 32
Needlepoint Canvas 14
Pewter Murano 30
Raw Linen Dublin Linen 25
Rustico 14
White Aida 14
White Annabelle 28
White Belfast Linen 32
White Murano 30

## THREADS

### Balger Products
Kreinik Mfg. Co., Inc.
P.O. Box 1966
Parkersburg, WV 26101
(800) 537-2166

#8 Gold Balger Braid
085 Peacock Balger Blending
    Filament
014 Sky Blue Balger Blending
    Filament

### DMC Flosses and Threads
The DMC Corporation
Port Kearny Building #10
South Kearny, NJ 07032
(800) 688-8362

DMC Flower Thread
DMC #3 Pearl Cotton
DMC #5 Pearl Cotton

## MISCELLANEOUS

### Acrylic Paint
Delta Technical Coatings, Inc.
2550 Pellissier Place
Whittier, CA 90601
Attention: Customer Service
(800) 423-4135

### Batting and Stuffing
Fairfield Processing Corp.
P.O. Box 1157
Danbury, CT 06813-1157
(800) 243-0989

### Clock
Wheatland Crafts
834 Scuffletown Road
Simpsonville, SC 29681
(800) 334-7706

### Craft Glue
Aleene's
85 Industrial Way
Buellton, CA 93427
(800) 436-6143

### Perforated Paper
Willmaur Crafts
735 Old York Road
Willow Grove, PA 19090
(215) 659-8782

### Ribbon
C. M. Offray and Son, Inc.
360 Route 24
Chester, NJ 07930
(908) 879-4700

### Sewing Machine
Bernina of America
3500 Thayer Court
Aurora, IL 60504-6182
(708) 978-2500

# Cover Designs

## Fruit Motifs

### SAMPLE
All motifs were stitched on peach Lugana 25 over 2 threads. Fabric sizes will vary with number of motifs stitched.

### SAMPLE for Pear
The finished design size for 1 motif is 1" x 1¼".

| FABRICS | DESIGN SIZES |
|---|---|
| Aida 11 | 1⅛" x 1½" |
| Aida 14 | ⅞" x 1⅛" |
| Aida 18 | ⅝" x ⅞" |
| Hardanger 22 | ½" x ¾" |

### SAMPLE for Apple
The finished design size for 1 motif is 1" x 1⅜".

| FABRICS | DESIGN SIZES |
|---|---|
| Aida 11 | 1⅛" x 1½" |
| Aida 14 | ⅞" x 1¼" |
| Aida 18 | ⅝" x 1" |
| Hardanger 22 | ½" x ¾" |

### SAMPLE for Peach
The finished design size for 1 motif is ¾" x ¾".

| FABRICS | DESIGN SIZES |
|---|---|
| Aida 11 | ⅞" x ⅞" |
| Aida 14 | ¾" x ¾" |
| Aida 18 | ½" x ½" |
| Hardanger 22 | ½" x ½" |

### SAMPLE for Grapes
The finished design size for 1 motif is 1⅞" x 1⅝".

| FABRICS | DESIGN SIZES |
|---|---|
| Aida 11 | 2⅛" x 1⅞" |
| Aida 14 | 1¾" x 1⅜" |
| Aida 18 | 1⅜" x 1⅛" |
| Hardanger 22 | 1⅛" x ⅞" |

### SAMPLE for Strawberries
The finished design size for 1 motif is 1" x 1".

| FABRICS | DESIGN SIZES |
|---|---|
| Aida 11 | 1⅛" x 1⅛" |
| Aida 14 | ⅞" x ⅞" |
| Aida 18 | ⅝" x ¾" |
| Hardanger 22 | ½" x ⅝" |

**Stitches to Go On**
Frame a small mirror for your dressing table or surround your favorite photograph with this fruitful border. Use the individual motifs to make jelly jar lids and a matching bread cloth.

## Fruitful Border

### SAMPLE
Stitched on peach Lugana 25 over 2 threads, the finished design size is 8¾" x 11½". The fabric was cut 15" x 18".

| FABRICS | DESIGN SIZES |
|---|---|
| Aida 11 | 10" x 13" |
| Aida 14 | 7⅞" x 10¼" |
| Aida 18 | 6⅛" x 8" |
| Hardanger 22 | 5" x 6½" |

| Anchor | | | DMC | (used for sample) |
|---|---|---|---|---|

**Step 1:** Cross-stitch (2 strands)

| Anchor | | DMC | |
|---|---|---|---|
| 297 | | 743 | Yellow-med. |
| 303 | | 742 | Tangerine-lt. |
| 10 | | 352 | Coral-lt. |
| 11 | | 3328 | Salmon-dk. |
| 13 | | 349 | Coral-dk. |
| 47 | | 321 | Christmas Red |
| 42 | | 335 | Rose |
| 59 | | 326 | Rose-vy. dk. |
| 87 | | 3607 | Plum-lt. |
| 89 | | 915 | Plum-dk. |
| 101 | | 327 | Antique Violet-vy. dk. |
| 266 | | 3347 | Yellow Green-med. |
| 216 | | 367 | Pistachio Green-dk. |
| 357 | | 801 | Coffee Brown-dk. |

**Step 2:** Backstitch (1 strand)

| Anchor | | DMC | |
|---|---|---|---|
| 246 | | 319 | Pistachio Green-vy. dk. (leaves) |
| 403 | | 310 | Black (grapes) |

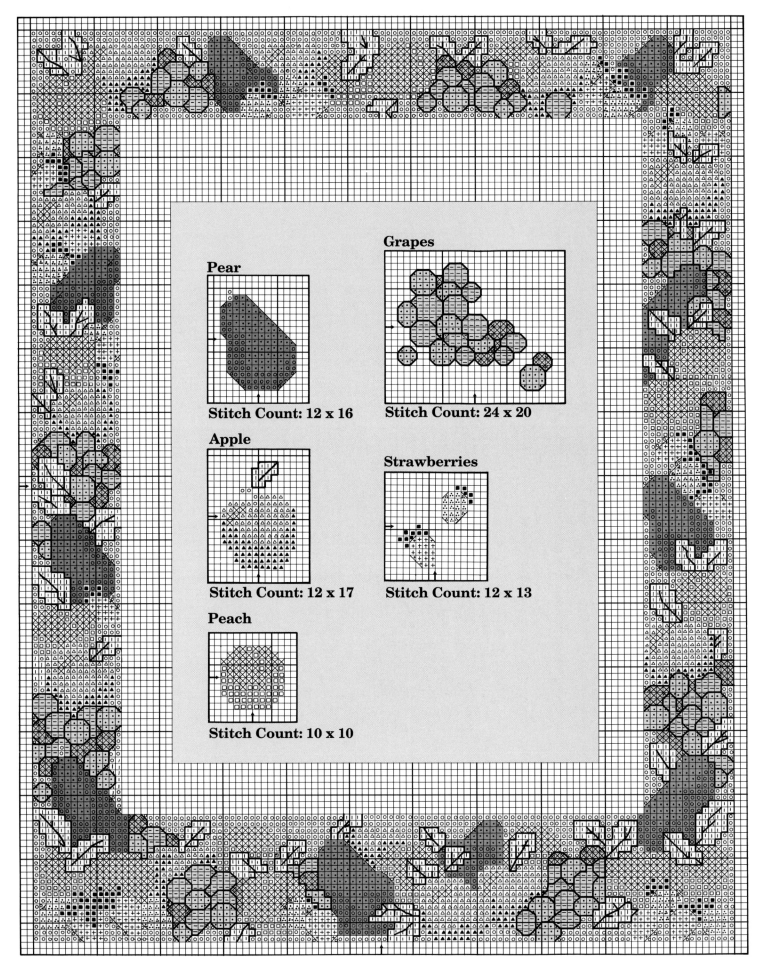

**Pear**

**Stitch Count: 12 x 16**

**Grapes**

**Stitch Count: 24 x 20**

**Apple**

**Stitch Count: 12 x 17**

**Strawberries**

**Stitch Count: 12 x 13**

**Peach**

**Stitch Count: 10 x 10**

**Stitch Count: 110 x 143**